GOD, CARS, & SOUVENIRS

GOD, CARS, & SOUVENIRS

ESSAYS

FRANCES NAIL

Frances Nail ♡

CITY DESK PRESS
AUSTIN, TEXAS

This book was written for my children,
Leslie Nail and Katherine Louise Nail,
and for my granddaughter, Carrie Luz Rodriguez,
in gratitude for their many eccentricities which,
while keeping me on the edge of my seat,
have given me so much to write about.

ALSO BY FRANCES NAIL

CROW IN THE HOUSE, WOLF AT THE DOOR

CONTENTS

TOO MUCH TO LOOK AT

for my mother

You sit down to pay bills
at a slab of red oak by the window.
On the lake below a boat writes a long message:
Work will wait. Take your time. Look at this.

You do. As you watch
the lake becomes the blue bottom
of a bowl. Your new house
full of shells and white doorknobs
balances on the bowl's high rim.
There is a canvas in the studio
but rabbits are in the rocks
as still as rocks and deer
browse in the cedars edging
toward your winter rye.
Pyracantha broadcasts hot orange.
Branches bob under a gray bird
flashing a white dot and dash
with its wings. A fish flips you
a finny tail, trying to snap
you out of it. You try to think
about cooking supper.
A crow ricochets from a distant tree.

Leslie Nail

FIGHTING

Tweedledum and Tweedledee
Agreed to have a battle
For Tweedledum said Tweedledee
Had spoiled his brand new rattle.

Lewis Carroll

Why do we fight? I know why I fought as a child. I wanted to be a boy something terrible and boys fought, so I was a fighter of the worst kind for a time when I was five. If a boy from Sixth or Eighth Street appeared on Seventh Street, he had to account for himself or he would be wrestled to the ground and dragged about a bit by the boys. I don't know why.

One of my earliest memories is of a fight (or maybe it wasn't) with Jack Miller, a handsome, blond boy about my size. He wandered out of the alley from Eighth Street. I only remember sitting on him and holding him down while the Seventh Street gang urged me on. I swaggered around all day with my much practiced boy walk. I wish I couldn't remember it; I hope Jack doesn't. And I made Cullen Chapman cry in a boxing ring wearing gloves that reached to our elbows. But the worst memory I have is of hitting Winifred Jane Tarver.

Janie's parents had moved to California, where she was born. They came back home and built a California bungalow on Seventh Street, unique in the little Pan-handle town of Memphis. The first time I saw Janie she was standing on the Moores' driveway. About four years old, she couldn't account for herself, so I, having only fought boys, took a different approach. I slapped her, hard. Janie began to cry. Naomi Moore saw it and hollered out her kitchen window, "Go home, Toot, and behave yourself!" Toot was an apt name for me at that time; I deserved it. I went crying home and gave up fighting. It was mean and I knew it and I hated it. I pray that Janie has forgotten it. I loved her.

But I was still jealous of the boys. My brother John, two years older, got to do things that I couldn't be-cause I was a little girl. W.R. Landis would come from the country to spend the night with us on a Friday night. Early the next morning, John and W.R. would walk to the Landis farm. The minute we were up I would begin to beg, "Please, please, please let me go!" "No," Ma would say, "you're too little." She meant, "You're a girl." The minute they left I would begin to wail.

I would walk around the house all morning, squalling and bawling. I could just see John and W.R. on their way. They would go down to the end of Seventh Street, cross Broom's Creek, go up through Broom's pasture, and out onto the road for four or five miles to the farm. There, they would strip off their clothes and swim in the horse tank under the windmill. Finally, my favorite thing (when I was there), they would stand on the edge of the tank and urinate in a graceful arcing stream off into the wild, blue yonder. How I envied them that skill and their apparatus that permitted it. I wasn't supposed to look when they were out of the water, but of course I did. Wouldn't have missed it for the world. No wonder I had such a case of penis envy. I wasn't allowed to swim naked. I had to keep my panties on. Boys could swim naked; girls could not. Oh, the injustice of it!

Actually, what they were doing on the edge of that tank was peeing. We didn't know the word *urinate*, and we weren't allowed to say the p-word. Our mother said it was common and vulgar. We said *tee-tee* until we were old enough to say *go to the bathroom*. I didn't hear people say the p-word much until I was grown. I thought they were common and vulgar. I guess I still do. I never say it. However, there's no other word that will do for boys on the rim of a horse tank.

One of those Saturdays at noon, Ma said, "Hush that crying and turn the radio on. It's time for your po-ems." Every Saturday a man with a heavenly voice would read poetry, mostly sad, over music played by a mournful organist. Still snuffling, I sat on the floor, leaned my head against our old Fada radio, and heard his first lines, "Don't cry, little girl, don't cry. I know they have broken your dolls and your playhouse, too." I fell back on the floor and howled, "I'm not a little girl and I don't have a playhouse!"

John was bad about fighting. He was little for his age, having had chorea, a form of rheumatic fever, caused by a strep throat. We called it then St. Vitus' dance. He was sick a lot and was only in the second grade when I started school. He was supposed to see that I got to school and home, but almost every day he picked a fight. Some big boy would be waiting for him a block from school. I would hold his books while he was drubbed and I would carry his books home while he limped crying along, our roles reversed. At last our cousin Chuck Jones, a big, strong boy John's age, rode herd on us. He would wait in the fighting spot, a mean look on his face. We were home free after that.

I quit envying boys a little later and began to play only with girls. I fell in love with the bootlegger's son at eleven and never looked back. But there was never a football game or dance in Memphis without a knock-down-and-drag-out by the boys. John grew to be a big football player and he would have been great, but he was called Slugger because he was forever punching someone on the football field.

Boys were still at it after we moved to Lubbock and I was in Texas Tech. I was leaving a dance with my beau, Paul Nail, and his fraternity brothers and their dates, when a boy from another fraternity came up and hit Paul in the mouth, knocking him to the pavement. It was a hit and run. We picked Paul up, crammed ourselves (four couples) into somebody's daddy's car, and drove to the Chicken Shack on Avenue Q, where we ordered French-fried onions. We ate the onions while one of the girls held ice to the big knot on Paul's head and I kept the blood wiped off his mouth. We discussed what was to be done. With the girls saying "No, no, no!" the boys wanted to gather up their club brothers, chase down the other fraternity, and have a big battle. But they left it to Paul. Paul was not a fighter; he couldn't have weighed much more than a hundred and forty pounds, though six feet tall, and he was also intelligent. He was mad about me and I told him if he fought that idiot I would never speak to him again. Paul said, "Let's go home," and so we did. That's the way it was and has always been, nationally, internationally, and locally—the big, fat bullies attack the skinniest. Dumb then, and dumb now.

But the biggest brawl I have ever seen was after the war. I had worked at the air bases during the war and had come back to school when the boys came home. You would think they would have been tired of fighting. No, not yet. A bunch of us, several couples, were going to the old Cotton Club out on the Slaton Highway to hear Jack Teagarten, his big band and his wonderful trombone. This was not an easy undertaking. The boys had to have ten bucks for two tickets and somebody had to go to Amarillo or Big Spring to buy booze. Finally, we were all there for the big night, dressed to the nines, the boys in coats and the girls all glamorous, drinking our expensive whiskey, dancing and having a wonderful time.

I had been going out with a sweet boy named Russell Gill. I called him Gill. He called me Pocahontas, Poke for short. He had been a prisoner of the Japanese and was back at Tech, trying to patch himself together. The Gills lived just down the street from us. But I didn't have a date with him that night, I was with Red Amonett, a big, red-headed football player. Sitting near us was Gill's sister and her husband and a young lieutenant, still in his uniform.

When Red excused himself and went to the restroom, Gill's sister and husband brought the lieutenant over to introduce him to me. We were chatting when Red came back. He walked up, hit the poor husband in the face and punched him to the floor. He then turned to the lieutenant, but he had fled.

A sort of insanity surged across that crowd. In one crazy instant, every boy at our table and the neighboring tables began to hit anyone within reach. The tables were overturned, glasses broken, bottles rolling around. Mounds of boys gone insane—without an enemy in the crowd—were rolling around on the floor with the bottles, pounding one another.

Then, with my back against the wall, I saw the strangest thing. A tall, pretty girl in a long, low-cut dress jumped on one of the fighting heaps. She was pulling hair, slapping, kicking and slashing with her high, spike heels, scratching and screaming. "Has she gone mad?" I wondered. No, they were on her mink coat.

In what seemed like hours, but was probably only twenty minutes, we found ourselves in a daze on the parking lot, money gone, whiskey gone, clothes torn and bloodied, and the great music denied us. With a long, plaintive note from Teagarten's trombone wafting after us on that lonesome highway, we drove slowly home, poorer and sadder, but no wiser.

I dreaded so to call the Gills' house the next day, to see if the son-in-law had lived. I felt responsible because Red had started the fight. I was relieved to hear Gill's voice answer. He was such a funny guy. He spoke pure dee Texsis, somewhat exaggerated for effect. Gill said, "Well, his face is all swole up, his eyes plumb black, his jaw looks kinda strange, and somp'ins wrong with one of his laigs, but he'll be all right." I apologized profusely. "Oh, you couldn't hep it, Poke," he said. "Whiskey done it."

Maybe so. I don't know if whiskey done it. To this day, I don't know whut done it.

JUNIOR HIGH DAYS

Maybe the devil made me do it. What else would have possessed me to chew up an art gum eraser? To sticky smithereens? And to hit dear Mr. Keaton with them? In the face!?

Mr. Keaton, the love of my life, was my fifth-grade teacher. Or was it sixth? Did he teach history or arithmetic? For the life of me, I can't remember. I can only remember Mr. Keaton. His skin was tan, his chin cleft, his eyes brilliant blue, and he had a darling shock of unruly, blond hair. With his white shirts, ties, and coats, he was so tweedy and English looking that if he even glanced my way I almost melted into a puddle on the classroom floor. I was not alone; most of the girls sat through class gazing into his eyes, their minds completely blank.

Poor Mr. Keaton. They might just as well have sent a lamb to teach wolves as to send such a young and handsome man to teach girls who had just learned how delicious it is to long for love. We yearned not for sex, but for romance, a different and more dangerous thing. I sat dreaming in his class every day, studying his eyebrows, eyes, nose, mouth, ears, and the cute way he waved his darling arms and hands to explain things. Whatever they were. I dreamed, of course, that he would give up everything for me and that we would run away and live happily ever after.

And that is the reason I chewed up the eraser and hit Mr. Keaton. I waited until the bell rang, gathered my books in my right hand, the wet eraser clutched in my left. Just as I went through the door, I turned back and threw the spitty bits at Mr. Keaton. He was tilted back in his chair and almost fell backward. They told me. I didn't see it; I was running too fast.

I thought he would come after me, take me by the arm (oooh) and lead me back to class, where he would keep me in for an hour. An hour all alone with Mr. Keaton was worth almost anything. Drat. It didn't happen that way. For one thing, I hadn't been prepared to be frightened out of my wits. He didn't run after me, but sent a kid who said, "Mr. Keaton said for

you to get yourself right back here! Boy, is he mad!"
And so, I lied. I said that I had aimed at Joyce Duren,
but she had moved. Joyce had been pelting the back
of my head with bits of her eraser (which gave me the
idea) and I knew he had seen it. But he didn't buy it.
And durn, there was also a boy being kept in. Mr.
Keaton pointed out to us a donkey staked out on the
golf course across the street and he told us to stay in
the classroom until we could no longer see that donkey, meaning until dark. And then, alas, Mr. Keaton
went home.

Billy Ed Thompson came in a little while and took his
donkey home. So we went home and I was glad. I
didn't know how I would ever explain to my ma if I
came in at dark. As it was, I told her the lie. I knew
even then that there are things which should not be
told, and that a lie can be kinder than the truth.

Poor Mr. Sweatt was nothing like Mr. Keaton. I'm not
real sure if his name was Sweatt, or if I have given it
to him because he was always wiping his brow with a
big handkerchief. He was a large, pale man with dark,
receding hair and cheerful, nervous ways. At least, he
was cheerful at first. It seems to me that he taught
math or was trying to in the seventh grade. He didn't
appeal to us and we sat there like a pack of hounds,
waiting for him to waver or blink. When he did, we
began to pass notes, talk, giggle, throw paper airplanes, and the boys would stroll around after Mr.

Sweatt said, "Sit down!" This caused him to keep them after school for punishment, three whacks with a paddle per boy. With every blow, the boys howled and pretended to be dying, until Mr. Sweatt, terribly aggravated, turned beet red. It's a wonder he didn't have a stroke. I know this because the girls were crouched outside under the windows, peeking in. With every whack, we rose up like a Greek chorus and gave a little shriek.

Poor Mr. Sweatt, he never came back to junior high or any school that I know of in Memphis, Texas. He didn't leave teaching forever, for I read about him after we had all come through that fit of madness called junior high, now middle school, and he and his twin brother were being extolled somewhere as brilliant and innovative teachers. Imagine two Mr. Sweatts.

Only those with iron wills should be sent to teach us just as we discover that we do not have to do what we're told, when we are yearning for romance or something that we know not of, and we are certain that we are the funniest people that were ever born. God help the weak soul who comes onto this scene.

The women teaching in junior high had it easier. For one thing, they were on to us. And they were not amused. I loved Beth Lemons, who taught geography and English. She married Shug, a handsome, sweet man, and she was sweet, also. She was Choctaw, with fair skin, big, dark, shining eyes, and coal black hair pulled back in a bun. We called her Miz Lemons. She asked us for more than we could do and leaned on us until we did it. I cannot remember one person ever misbehaving in her class. She had us writing plays in English class and I think she invented the concept of projects. For geography, I carved a Mexican pueblo from Ivory soap, flat-roofed houses, cactus, right down to the obligatory Mexican asleep under his sombrero. I painted them and mounted them on a board with sand and plants and roads and such. Miz Lemons loved it and when she had visitation day for mothers to come and view the projects, she sent a special note home with me. She knew my mother; she knew an old Indian when she saw one. Beth was twenty-eight; Ma was fifty.

My mother's philosophy was that school was school and home was home and never the twain should meet. But even Ma, who obeyed nobody, obeyed Miz Lemons. While Ma admired my pueblo, she was sick of it. She had watched all of the soap she could afford at five cents a bar flying off the kitchen table for weeks in tiny shavings, while I sat with a knife like a small maniac in a blizzard. When she washed the table after supper, it foamed. At school, I was real proud of her. She smiled, didn't look bored at all, but acted like an ordinary, pleasant mother. Hard for her, but she did it for Miz Lemons. With Miz Lemons, you had no choice.

I was a Ready Writer, an essay writer who competed in county and regional meets, because Miz Lemons said I must. I brought home four blue ribbons in two years because she was waiting for them.

I always thought Beth Lemons was Chief Gardner's daughter. I guess because Beth was half Indian and Chief Gardner full blood. They were the only Indians I knew, except my mother who was twice removed from a Cherokee. I was shocked to learn from Beth's obituary that her maiden name was Moreland and she came from Oklahoma at twenty in 1928 to teach school. She married Shug in 1930 when I was in the first grade. I have had the notion that she was born in Memphis and that Chief Gardner was her father for sixty-five years. No matter, to me she will always be the daughter of Chief Gardner.

A picture of Jess Gardner in a Hall County book shows him in 1920 as a young man, a tall, handsome Indian not much older than Beth. When I had my dealings with Chief Gardner, he was older, wider, taller, and forbidding as he towered over his meat counter. He had a butcher shop on the east side of the square. My mother loved to buy meat from him, but it was an intricate process. She would order a roast on the phone and send me to get it. A big roast. She would unwrap the roast, take one look and start roaring around the kitchen. Then she would say, "Take this back to Chief Gardner and tell him that I wouldn't feed it to the dogs!" I walked very, very slowly until I stood below Chief Gardner's tall counter. In a small voice, I said, "My mother doesn't like this roast." The Chief said nothing, expressionless as always. He reached his great arm over the counter and plucked up that roast with one huge hand. In a minute or so, he handed me a new package. "Take her this one," he said, and he almost smiled. I scurried out and made the eight blocks home with the twelve pound roast, like carrying a baby. Ma would slowly and silently unwrap the roast. It was a ceremony. Finally she would say, "Now, that's more like it!"

I know, now, that the Chief sent the same roast back that I returned. It was an Indian game they played, the Chief on the square and the squaw down on South Seventh Street. It was an Indian game or maybe an Indian dance, the Dance of the Roast. If so, I was the dancer.

If Beth Lemons taught me how to make a sentence and how to write an essay, Zady Belle Walker taught me to love writing. Not the physical act of it, which she taught, but the hearing of it. As a reward for good work, she would read in her marvelous voice a long, unusual story, one we would never have known, holding us spellbound until the bell rang.

Zady Belle Walker was not a glamorous woman; she was heavyset, a stolid person. Her dark eyes would have been soulful, except they were always laughing. She had dark hair, beautiful hands, and she moved through the classroom with such grace. She was beautiful to me. She taught art and writing, the Spencerian method. Holding a pen staff properly, using the muscles in our forearms for movement, after all the straight lines and ovals, we were to write beautiful, perfect letters, slanting to the right. Some did; I didn't. Peggy George excelled and still writes in that beautiful manner today. She had to; she was Zady's baby sister. I reverted to my backhand. We wrote letters in those days, mailing them with three-cent stamps. I practiced my peculiar form, putting circles over the i's, until it was sufficiently exotic for my pen pals. I still hold my pen properly.

Zady Belle taught us to paint with watercolor and we made a book, bound in black, with pages on color, a color wheel, and studies of perspective. Mine disappeared years ago, though I still search for it. But Zady Belle changed my life, inadvertently, with a Van Gogh print that she brought home from Europe. No attention was paid to art in those days by anyone I knew except Zady Belle. We all had dreary little prints on the walls—*The End of the Trail*, the Indian slumped on his horse at sunset, and *Harp of the Winds*, poplars in a row—sold to us all by a traveling salesman. The only real painting I can remember, though there may have been some, was a big oil of *Custer's Last Stand* that hung with all of its gore in Old Man Franks' garage behind his desk. Every soul in it was bleeding to death except Custer, heroic and brandishing his sword on his big horse. Mammy Franks wouldn't allow it in the house.

As was the custom long ago, especially during the Depression, everyone stayed home until home grew too small. Zady Belle lived across the street from the junior high with her parents, married brothers and wives, younger sisters, and some children off and on. A family of teachers and coaches. In those days and in our homes of no privacy, we didn't shout or knock, we just wandered in, as I did one day, looking for Peggy George. I called and started to sit down when I saw on the opposite wall such an amazing thing that I sank onto the couch.

Hanging in that ordinary Memphis living room was a large and fine print of Armand Roulin, the postmaster's son. Van Gogh painted it in Arles before he killed himself. Armand Roulin was a beautiful man in his blue hat and yellow coat, gazing out from a pale blue ground. Zady Belle had framed it perfectly and it hung with wires from the picture molding. As in a museum. I had never seen a museum, but I knew that painting to be the most sophisticated thing that I would ever see.

After that day, when I went for Peggy George I went early, as to a shrine, so I could meditate on Armand

Roulin. Zady Belle had just taught us to paint with watercolor and I strove for perfection. But here was this sloppy-looking painting, the background just smeared, funny strokes all over the face, and the yellow coat outlined in black, its folds just smears of green paint. Yet, there he was, Armand Roulin, a living, breathing soul, looking at me with his beautiful, enigmatic eyes. And the strangest thing of all, Armand's eyes, though darker, had the very same expression as Mr. Keaton's.

I never think of my junior high days without counting my blessings. We had no guns or drugs or sex or any knowledge of them. Had we known, we would have wanted them. We were the last innocent generation, allowed in our time to be children. Our entertainment was Jack Benny and his jokes and that wonderful Amos and Andy. Those guys had us rolling on the floor. Our misbehavior involved paper airplanes. Our music was patriotic, old hymns, Frank Sinatra with his eternal message of love, and old cowboy songs about old cowboys dying without their mothers.

Beth Lemons died last March at eighty-nine. She had children and grandchildren and she died an honored woman. Zady Belle Walker gave her life to teaching. She was a principal and famous among teachers. She made me long so to paint that against all odds, I painted one way or another for sixty marvelous years. She was a teacher of dreams. Zady Belle lives in

Amarillo. She is old and she is blind. Her handwriting is still better than mine.

We loved our teachers. I still do. Even Mr. Sweatt. And somewhere back in a bright corner of my old brain, I keep Mr. Keaton. I see him once in a while, that beautiful blue-eyed man, tilted back in his chair in his tweed coat, and I still plan to run away with him. As soon as he finds me.

CARS

I was twenty-six years old before I learned to drive, but cars come on strong in my old memories—someone else's cars, since we never owned one. The Lord will provide, as my fundamentalist sister would say. But the Lord did not provide. My husband, Paul, and I, born two of the poorest children in Texas, worked like dogs for two years after we married, saving to buy our first car. We were born not long after Henry Ford's assembly line, when he made the Model-T, the first car owned by ordinary people, changing our lives forever.

The first long trip I ever made in one was from Memphis to Kosse, my parents' hometown down in Limestone County, about four hundred miles. Four hundred miles and fifty years away from the life I knew in

Memphis. We called Kosse East Texas, though it's not far from Waco. In Kosse I watched Auntie cook on a wood stove and stir a huge black pot of turnip greens hanging over her kitchen fireplace. Her kitchen was tacked on to the end of the old dogtrot house, its hall an open porch through the middle. Auntie became my grandmother when her sister died, leaving nine children. My mother was the middle child at fifteen, four about grown, and five very young down to the new baby that survived my grandmother's death. My mother worshipped Auntie and Uncle, Ophelia and Zachary Taylor Williams, as did all of her brothers and sisters and all of their children and hers, including me. I still have the absolute joy I felt when Uncle picked me up and put me in the back of his wagon with Bob and John and some of our cousins. He kissed us little ones. I felt like I had been blessed by the Pope, or would have if I'd ever heard of him.

Uncle took us in the back of his wagon down old dirt roads, some with intertwined trees overhead, tunnels through deep woods, now gone. Staring at the horses and the trees and at Uncle with his mustache, his sweet, blue eyes and shining white hair, survivor of the Civil War, we were overcome and went silently through the woods, the only sounds the horses' hoofs, the rattles of the old wagon, and the birds.

And so we came to Aunt Ruth's. Aunt Ruth was a great but poor woman. She had only iced tea, butter, and roasting ears for lunch that day. Roasting ears, I think, were ears left too long in the field, big ears with big, tough kernels and the truest corn taste possible, when corn was corn before the flavor was tenderized out of it. We went out with Ruthie, cut those ears, shucked them, and she put them covered with butter in her wood stove until they were as brown as toast. We were silent again as we gnawed through those ears like a bunch of squirrels. I yearn for them yet.

I seem to be having one of my crazy spells. I was trying to recall the old cars I knew and the places I went in them, but found myself going down an old red dirt road in a wagon behind Uncle's horses to Aunt Ruthie's corn patch. Memory cannot be trusted. It can take you down bad roads, just ruts, to dark, unknown places with no way to turn around.

Never mind. It was June in 1929 when my cousin E.B. Lowery came for us in his Model-T. He left Kosse before dawn and arrived long after midnight. We were waiting up for him, our clothes bundled up, our sacks full of food. Before that time, I have a vague memory of going to Kosse on the train. All I recall from that trip is my brother John urinating on the tracks in Fort Worth and my mother yelling and grabbing him. She was frightened of the trains, not embarrassed. Nothing embarrassed that woman.

So I must have met E.B. earlier, before he got out of his Model-T and staggered exhausted into the house that night. E.B. was the best looking man that ever walked the face of this earth. He would have put Paul Newman to shame. About twenty, he had big steel-blue eyes, olive skin, a sweet mouth, and he wore a homburg hat. I was only five and knew nothing of swooning, but when I looked at E.B. I had a sudden weakening of the knees and sank to the floor. Ma fed him and we lay down for a while, got up before day-light, loaded the Model-T, and took off on our long day's journey.

Ma sat in front with E.B. Bob, John, and I sat wide-awake and big-eyed in the back seat. We had only made ten miles when we came to the Prairie Dog Town Fork of the Red River. We knew it was the Prairie Dog Fork, but we called it Red River. We had never seen the big one. They were building a bridge over the river and we had to detour through the river bed. We had only begun to cross when we had a flat. Alas, for E.B. He was always dressed up. He took off his hat and his tie and tackled the flat in the deep sand. We got out in the dark to lighten the load as he jacked up the car. Ma held a flashlight while we chil-dren played in the sand, nuttier than fruitcakes. We made that long trip, shoes and clothes full of Red River sand, eating out of our sacks, through Chillecothe, Quanah, on to Fort Worth and down through Hillsboro, Hubbard, Mexia, and Groesbeck to

Kosse, where we spilled out of the Model-T in the middle of the night at Aunt Sister's house.

We were met by a crowd of kin who were kissing, shouting and crying, hugging and patting us from head to toe. I had never seen anything like it and didn't know why. But my mother did. At that time, she was the only child who had left Kosse except for Aunt Gus, who followed her to Memphis, and Zack, who only went to Mexia. It was a Limestone County thing. Still goes on at Kosse reunions, though most of the kissers and shouters are gone. We are all nomads now. We still kiss and hug but we seldom shout and cry. We have become accustomed to absence.

I don't know why I can't remember how we got home. Maybe it was so bad I blanked it out. John got very sick in Kosse. He had fallen out of a pear tree before we left, cracking his pelvic bone. He knew he was hurt bad, but he hid it from Ma because of the trip. He had osteomyelitis, an infection of the bone. How he got over it, with no money and no antibiotics, a long time after our ride in the Model-T, is a long, sad story.

Another Model-T tale I don't recall because I wasn't born yet or was a baby, but I tell it as Ma told it. My cousin Chuck Jones doesn't remember it this way, but what could he know? He was sitting in the floorboard with his foot on the gas. I trust Ma's memory. It happened at my Aunt Gus's house. Everyone had come for Sunday dinner at noon and there was a Model-T parked in front. My sister Bob and Chuck, precocious children about six and four, decided to drive it. I don't know how they started it, but Bob was driving and Chuck was a boy who could do anything. Maybe he cranked it. They took off and went around the block, Bob steering, Chuck feeding the gas. They made it once around the block before it was discovered that they were gone in the car. The chase began.

The men ran as fast as they could after the car on its second time around. They ran out of breath and didn't catch it. They were standing in the street, huffing and puffing and praying, when here came the car again. This time, they jumped on the running board and stopped it. Bob and Chuck were always doing things like that. There are no running boards today; don't leave your key in the car.

The first car I ever loved was Grace Duke's car. I wish I could remember what it was, but everyone who knew is gone. Grace was a widow and it was her husband's car, but she learned to drive it. How, I don't know, as she was a short, round woman with very short legs. John and I had to clamber up onto the running board and then climb to get in the great back seat. The car was huge and black with black leather seats and maybe a canvas top. It was open in the summer, but in the winter Grace hung celluloid windows on little hooks.

Didn't help much. She came for us every Sunday afternoon after my brother died to take us to the cemetery, always an exhilarating ride because Grace didn't have much control over that car. She could only jab at the clutch and brake with the tips of her little toes. It swooped around curves and tore down the stretches until it slid to a halt at the cemetery. When we arrived, weak-kneed, Grace to tend to her husband's grave and Ma to Freddy's, John and I would head for the angels.

Memory plays such tricks on us. Until we buried my father I thought there were three angels. There are only two. I thought they were eight feet tall; they are about five. I thought Mr. Hawthorne had three wives and had ordered from France a marble angel each time he lost one. He only did this twice. I didn't know Mr. Hawthorne and he had not yet joined his wives when John and I played with his angels.

While we played with angels, we could hear Ma singing over Freddy's grave in her mourning voice, "I come to the garden alone, while the dew is still on the roses." There were no roses on Freddy's grave on that dry hillside. I wanted him to have an angel, but we couldn't even buy him a stone.

We would climb Henrietta's angel, hang on to her wings, and stare into her strange eyes. Henrietta was born in St. Nazaire, France, in 1896 and died in

Memphis in 1926. She didn't last long in Memphis. Maybe it was culture shock. On the base of her stone is written "The Rose from No Man's Land." So she was a war bride from World War One, which we called the Great War. It wasn't great. How little we knew. Oveta's angel was kneeling on one knee. We would sit on her knee and feel that an angel was holding us on her lap. I haven't had that feeling since. Oveta died in 1935 at twenty-four. On the base of her stone it says "Mother is your best friend." I wonder why? Mr. Hawthorne lies between the angels. He was a sergeant in the war. His name was Will.

I've forgotten what the car looked like that Fats Kunkler drove when he ran over me. I can still see its bumper and grille. In the first grade, I was walking home to lunch when I stepped onto Main Street just as Fats turned the corner. I grabbed the bumper as I went down and was dragged over the red bricks until Fats could stop. I jumped up and took off like a scared rabbit. Fats chased me, but with his weight, he was no match. I ran down the nearest alley, zigging and zagging all the way home. He thought he had killed me and that I had run into the alley to die, like a wounded cat. He spent too much time in the alley, peering under bushes.

When I got home, I sat with my back to the wall, saying nothing. After all her warnings, I didn't want Ma to know I was dumb enough to get run over.

When she brought my plate she said, "Child, what is wrong? You look awful." "I don't feel very good," I replied. She sent me to bed, but before she could come to see about me, Fats was there, moaning, crying, and telling her he'd killed me and couldn't find me. He was a happy man when he saw me. The hide all scraped off my back, I was covered up to the ears, trying to hide the evidence. I felt bad about bleeding on the sheets.

There was a filling station on the corner where I was run over and on its drive was a two-toned roadster with orange wire wheels and a rumble seat. It had married into our family with my sister Loisie's husband, who worked in the station. I was so proud of that car. When school first started I would stand on the corner telling every child that passed that the car belonged to my brother-in-law until John would drag me home. I was looking at the roadster when poor Fats' old Chevy ran me down.

Teenagers didn't own cars and there were no driving schools, but they were taught to drive as soon as their feet reached the pedals. They didn't have licenses, but they drove just the same, most at about thirteen. My friend Peggy George Walker would get her father, Red's, car on a Sunday afternoon when we were about fourteen. Now, Red was a man you wouldn't want to mess with. As wide as he was tall, he had red hair, a red face, and a temper that fit him.

We would take his car and some borrowed cigarettes out the highway to Estelline, smoking all the way. We rode back with the windows down in the dead of winter, the frigid wind whipping us unmercifully, to rid the car of the smoky smell. Red would have killed us faster than the cigarettes.

I remember Annie Ruth Williams learning to drive, though I wasn't there. Her daddy, Vernon, was a partner with my dad in a drugstore in Memphis. Annie Ruth and my sister Bob were both born in 1918. They were and are best friends. Annie Ruth became a sister to us when she was born. She looked like Elizabeth Taylor (and still does), with brilliant blue, sometimes green eyes, thick black hair, and long, black, fringy eyelashes. Her mother and daddy had the flu during the terrible epidemic of 1918. My mother took Annie Ruth and, for weeks, nursed her along with Bob and she was bonded to us forever. They moved to Chillecothe where Vernon had his own drugstore until he died. We visited back and forth, especially Bob, who spent a lot of time there. She was there when Annie Ruth learned to drive, taught by her mother, Miss Eunice. I don't know why we called her Miss Eunice, we just did.

When Miss Eunice taught Annie Ruth to drive at eleven or twelve, Bob was in the back seat. Annie Ruth would careen around corners, screeching to stops, while Miss Eunice screamed over and over,

"ANN-NIE ROOOTH!" Then she lurched off in jumps and stops, Miss Eunice's voice reduced to a pleading whisper, "Annie Roooth, Annie Roooth." Even today, when we see Anne Tabor, as she is known, or hear her voice on the phone, we yell, "ANN-NIE ROOOTH!"

My daddy never had the slightest desire for a car. He was afraid of them. He never got over horses and buggies. He walked until he grew too old to walk, in Lubbock, where he rode buses and cabs. When he rode in a car he sat by the door, his hand on the latch, ready to jump out. Ma, on the other hand, grieved all her life because she didn't have one. No car ever left without her, no matter its destination, whether she was invited or not. If I heard her say once, I heard it a million times, "If I just had a car." I'm glad she didn't have one. She had no patience. She would have been a demon driver, switching lanes, giving people the finger, and shouting curses.

I yearned for cars, also, until my husband and I finally bought our first—a sleek, black, two-door '49 Chevy, a glorious car. We drove all over Houston on the first day and got in bed too excited to sleep. About twelve, Paul got up and left the room. I asked, "Where are you going?" "I am going," he said, "to see how the interior lights work when the door is opened." I followed him.

I have had many cars since that day, but I seldom leave home in one without subconsciously praising God for it. I am nearly old, but I drive all over Texas wherever and whenever I want to go. Oh, I do love cars. There's no freedom like having one, going when and where you please, coming home when you please. We need to give them up, but until we have trains, buses, subways, and cheap cabs to be hailed on the street as Europe has, we will drive our cars. Ye shall know the car and the car shall make you free.

My mother, had she owned a car, would have been one of those old drivers that people complain about, though she would never have driven too slowly. She could have driven until she was nearly ninety, until we pried her from her car and took her keys to keep her home. I will be the same, should I live so long. My kids, one day, will have to drag me from mine, kicking and howling and hanging for dear life to the heavenly steering wheel.

DREAM

I had the craziest dream. Most of my dreams leave me, unless I write them down or recall them in detail as soon as I wake. But this one was so vivid, with such bright colors, that I not only didn't forget it, but *can't* forget it. It was funny, while my dreams are more often dead serious, if not downright weird. It was about a competition and I am a sucker for those. To win the money, you had to show up with a driver to chauffeur you around in a big, baby blue Cadillac. While being driven through the city, which was Houston, I was to record my impressions of the car, telling what I thought about it in detail. When we returned, my driver was to record her feelings about driving it.

For my driver I chose Kay Owen, my daughter Katy's childhood friend. In the dream she was thirteen. Seated in the blue velvet back seat, I was handed a microphone and we drove off. Before I could say a word about the car, a voice from a speaker asked why I had chosen my driver. I said, "Well, Kay is a great travel writer. She and her sisters traveled in the back seat of an elderly car called the Blue Bomber, her parents driving them all over the United States and most of Mexico, Kay writing odd letters to Katy from all those far places which we never saw." This part of the dream about the Owens' travels was really true.

And then I started my recording. "This seat is soft and luxurious, such a pretty blue, and it has a grand ash-tray." I hated that ashtray, because in real life I had just quit smoking. I was going on and on about the car, when suddenly, I said, "Oh, Kay, this reminds of the time you and Katy sneaked out in the middle of the night and were walking around Meyerland and the police picked you up and took you downtown. I guess because I am in the back seat being chauf-feured. And do you remember, Kay, you were in a back brace reaching from your chin to your waist, and when they put you in the patrol car they slammed the door on your thumb? And Paul and Ed had to go downtown at four in the morning to get y'all out of jail? And weren't they mad!" Then I fell into a laughing heap and laughed and laughed. I don't know if this would have been so funny in the dream had it not been a scene from real life.

I pulled myself together, though, and said to the microphone that this car, of course, was nothing like a patrol car, that actually we were just floating over the road in it. And then it was raining, not just a shower, but one of those Houston rains that flood the streets from curb to curb. I was beginning to describe the way the car drove through the water, not chugging, but floating along, when I looked into the street to see the water rushing by against the curb. And in the water, swimming like mad, was a rat. Not a big ugly gray rat, but a pretty little brown one. "Oh, Kay! I wish you could see this little rat. He sees me . . . he's waving and waving his little hand . . . no . . . wait a minute . . . he's not waving, he's drowning."

I looked at that gorgeous ashtray and wished to God I had a cigarette. I tried once again to speak to the microphone about the car. I managed to say that you would never find a rat in this elegant car, but after that, it was hopeless. I broke up in hysterical laughter every time I said, "This car. . . . " I gave up and flailed around in that great back seat laughing and crying, like Katy and Kay used to do when they rolled on the floor, laughing uncontrollably over nothing. "Kay," I finally asked, "do you remember when y'all were driving through the West in a barren place, looking for a spot to have lunch, and you came to this lovely green oasis, where you had your picnic at the sewage treatment plant in Jackass Flats? Or was it Mexican Hat?"

I woke up then, still laughing. The strangest thing about the dream was Kay. From the time she silently appeared and got behind the wheel, she said not one word and I never saw her face, only the back of her beautiful head and her long chestnut hair. When she was thirteen in real life, her mouth never closed.

After a while, I went smiling back to sleep. But as dark must follow light, I had another dream. Just as vivid, but drab, it was a terrible, gray dream that I can *not* forget, though a week has gone by. It was about my mother. I found her homeless and abandoned, living in an old, empty, ugly house, its windows all broken. It was cold and she was crying. But that is another dream.

THE OTHER DREAM

This dream, lacking color except for some blue shadows, was in grays and deep blacks. The only light in the dream was a cold white from snow. The dream was of an old house that I used to dream of only when it snowed. In those dreams, I never went inside the house. But in this dark dream, I did.

In the kitchen of the sad, dirty house, I found my mother sitting on an old straight chair by a cold woodstove. The windows were all broken and it was *cold* in that house. I asked her what she was doing there and who had broken the windows. She shook her head and cried. When my mother lived, only death made her cry. And the strangest thing, there was a telephone on the wall like our first one that hung in our hall, when we still talked to operators. I wanted my sister Lois, who left this world twenty years ago. "Ida Mae," I said to the operator, "get me Lois." Lois answered. "Loisie," I said, "I've found Ma in this old house full of broken windows. She is homeless and she's crying." "I know," replied Loisie, hanging up.

Fortunately, I am a cognitive dreamer and can shuck off nightmares. I simply say, "This is only a dream and I don't have to put up with it." But I did have to put up with this dream and could not forget it, because I knew that old house and I knew who broke the windows.

J.K. and I did it, but J.K. was not to blame. I was often in trouble when I played with J.K., but I was always the one thinking of things to do and J.K. was always just nodding his head.

We were five years old when we broke the windows in that dreadful house. An abandoned house, its tenants never stayed long. It was a sad house, having absorbed so much sadness from so many sad people. It was at the corner of Sixth Street across from Janie's grandpa's house and catty-cornered across the intersection from Mammy Franks'. It didn't fit the neighborhood, unpainted and uncared for in any way, no heat or lights. But I am making excuses, trying to explain my craziness. J.K. and I played around the house when it was empty, but we never went inside. We were afraid of it. One day, when it had new occupants, we saw a boy's face in the kitchen window. We knocked on the door. It barely opened, but we could see a woman's face back in the shadow. "Can your little boy come out?" we asked. "No, he cain't," she said, closing the door. J.K. and I, startled and confused, stood around a few minutes, asking loudly, "Whut kind of a little boy cain't come out? Why cain't he?" It made us, though, so uneasy, we took off in a run to my house where we sat on the steps, eating cookies to calm our nerves.

I think it was when that family moved out that J.K. and I broke the windows. When the house was empty, we would play with some fire pokers we found under the back steps. We used them like swords, swinging and slashing around in the yard at bushes and such. We always put them back. They were ours. One day, after we took our pokers for our fencing game, I said, "J.K., there is something awful in this old house. I can see it in the windows, watching us. We've got to get it out." J.K. nodded. "Watch me," I said. I ran and broke a window, shrieking like a banshee. J.K. broke the next one, though I think I did all of the shrieking as we ran around the house, breaking every window. Then we threw the pokers to the ground and ran up the alley, scared spitless.

Now, Mammy Franks was watching us as we destroyed the windows. The village that it takes to raise a child didn't work that day. She called my mother to tell her what we had done. "In the name of God, woman," Ma shouted, "why didn't you stop them?" For one thing, Mammy wasn't fond of that old house. She thought the people who lived there off and on were squatters and they may have been. We were not yet familiar with the homeless. She also was suspicious of some tenants she thought were Gypsies. I imagine that Mammy was saying, "Go, kids, go!" as I committed my only crime that I can remember right off.

I got off easy. Ma was madder at Mammy Franks than she was at me. But I wasn't home free. She made me feel bad about what I had done, telling me the windows weren't likely to be replaced and how cold, oh how cold, that house would be next winter.

The windows were replaced . . . with cardboard. I tried not to look at them as I grew older, walking to Janie's grandpa's house, where she then lived. J.K. and I never played in the yard of the old house again. He moved to Colorado sometime after, and being innocent, I'm sure he never gave that house a thought. But I never got over it.

Around twelve I began to dream of it when snow fell, because one day, after Christmas but before New Year's, I walked out in a deep snow, the snow still falling. I remember putting on a pair of thick, cotton stockings over my shoes. I would have worn boots, if I'd had them. But our house was warm and bright with its big Christmas tree and smelled delicious from cookies and cakes and turkey and good things. I was on my way to Janie's, whose house was the same.

The old house had been empty for months, but as I reached the corner I stopped, as always. Oh, Lord. One weak, wan wisp of smoke was rising from the kitchen chimney. I stood in the beautiful falling snow, looking at those cardboard windows. I said to myself, "Oh, God! Someday I will fix those broken windows." I never did. That old house was gone before I had a dime.

I knew a photographer in Houston. Martha is all I remember of her name. She loved old, deserted houses and often drove into the country, searching them out. In the past, four generations might occupy a house. Martha thought the house absorbed the happiness or sorrow of the occupants. She could feel the "vibes," as she described it, as she took her pictures of old places. Once, she and her brother (I think it was her brother) were in a deserted house up in the Big Thicket, if I am remembering it right. I do remember the picture she took, through the glass in the front door. She said that they were uneasy when they came into the house and she was anxious to leave, but stopped to take the photo. At that moment, she said, they felt a terror and ran from the house in a panic. I wish I had bought her photograph, so I could see it once more. She thought she had a picture of a ghost and there was something seen through that door, something crouched down on the path at the edge of the woods that were creeping toward the house.

When you looked at it, there it was. But when you weren't looking, you couldn't remember what it looked like.

I took my granddaughter up to Kosse for a reunion of my mother's family when Carrie was nearly three. When we came home I took the road down to Troy, winding through the countryside so Carrie could see something other than the freeway. Going through the fields we came around a bend and saw a wonderful, old, abandoned farmhouse. It looked ancient. I explained to Carrie that many people, like us, had once lived in that house, but they had gone away. She wanted to go in it, but the weeds in the field were high; it was May, and the snakes were hungry. Next time, I said.

The next year, she still remembered that house. "Go down to Troy," she said and began to watch for the house as soon as we were on the road. When we came around the bend and saw it, she was very excited. "There it is! Stop! Gramma, we've got to go in the house. Please stop, I want to see it." Well. I stopped, but I didn't want to see it. It wasn't just the weeds and the snakes. It was the house. Its gloom reached across the field, chilling me, and I felt it calling to us. Carrie was a strange child, her senses so strong, she saw, heard, smelled, tasted, and touched everything as soon as she could walk. She sensed everything. "No, Carrie," I said, "we can't go in the house today." And I lit out for home. I did not like that house that wanted my baby.

I've never seen one of Martha's ghosts and there are few deserted houses left in the countryside. The malls and suburbs have taken most of them, but should you come across one somewhere in the woods or fields, be watchful for gloom or cheer. And be wary. That bleak house down on Sixth Street still haunts me in my dreams, when snow is falling. In the Hill Country I haven't been bothered with it much. So little snow. But sometimes at Christmas, when my house is warm and cheerful, I see as in a dream the broken windows, the little wisp of smoke, and the pale, puzzled face of the little boy, like Tiny Tim.

My Ghost of Christmas Past doesn't rattle chains, but looks at me over a cardboard window. It is the face of a little boy, a little boy who couldn't come out.

BEAUTIFUL BIRD

I heard some birds in the Basses' live oaks. It was a familiar sound, but I couldn't place it. Not a pretty song, but a rasping, creaking sound, as that of an old door with rusty hinges, opening and closing. The sun was going down over Lake Travis, that time of the day when everything glows and the light is magical, picking up the color from the lake and transforming every mundane thing into beauty.

I could see the Basses' oaks from my kitchen window and was trying to see the birds when a big black bird lit in one of my oaks, right above the window. At first I thought he was a small crow, but his neck was too short and his tail was wrong. He seemed in no hurry to leave, so I got my binoculars. When he came into focus, I gasped. What a magnificent creature!

He was ruffling up the magenta and purple feathers on his head. At the base of his neck there was a little green turning to a gleaming bronze on his back with tinges of gold. His breast and the top of his wing were pale, molten yellow, like gold and silver melted together. His eyes were sleepy and he settled and unsettled himself, as if getting ready to sleep in my tree. I was pleased, thinking maybe he would come back to sleep every night.

I watched him a long time and then took down my bird books. I searched through all of the big, exotic, iridescent birds. I couldn't find him. So turning to the blackbirds, my eye lit on the Common Grackle. A GRACKLE?! ARRRG! This bird was trying out my tree; tomorrow he would bring his friends. I could see a black cloud of grackles coming every night to the oaks, with their gaudy, neon getup, like a thousand technicolored demons glowing in the twilight, pooping all over the Basses and me and driving us mad with their mess and noise, now and forevermore.

I ran outside shouting. "Shoo! Scat! Get from here!" I clapped my hands and looked for something to bang on. The grackle wasn't afraid of me. He gave me a reproachful look, but didn't move. After I had made all of the noise I could, practically climbing the tree, he stood up and slowly and reluctantly flew away. He looked back as if to say, "Are you some kind of crazy woman, or whut?" I hollered after him, "Git outa here and don't come back, you ugly wretch!"

Beauty is in the eye of the beholder, before the truth is known.

THE BIRDS

My mother loved blue jays. Maybe because they are so ornery and noisy. She was an ornery, noisy woman. In the spring, when they are courting, jays make lovely, musical sounds, but in the fall they holler Jay! Jay! Jay! To Ma, it was a lonesome call. "Just listen to those old jays," she would say. "They know it's time to go." I suppose jays left Memphis in the fall. Winter was cold out there at the foot of the Llano Estacado, the Great High Plains that reach to Canada.

Ma loved all birds, especially mourning doves. She heard one at dawn, as my brother was dying. Ever after that morning she never heard one without pausing. "Do you hear that old dove?" she'd say. And when a mockingbird kept us awake on a summer night, she'd say, "Just listen to that old mockingbird!"

When I was a small child she had a canary. He was a great singer. When she took the cover off his cage in the morning he would begin to trill away. She loved that yellow bird. "Just listen to that!" she'd say. She thought it a miracle to have a bird's song in the house.

She had a crow, but that tale has been told. After the crow was gone she missed him so much she got a parakeet. A pretty bird, his name was Blue. She tried to teach him to talk. Blue said not one word to Ma, but no telling *what* Ma said to Blue. He probably couldn't bring himself to repeat it. She did teach him one bad trick. She would open his cage door and say, "Come out, Blue, and fight like a man!" The parakeet would come out of the cage like a torpedo and flog the living daylights out of anyone standing nearby.

He should have flogged Ma, but he always chose the unlucky, innocent soul. I was married and gone when she had Blue, but I did see him come out and fight. It was not a pretty sight. He was loose in the house most of the time and he left one day through an open door. She searched for that bird, endlessly calling his name, "Blue, Blue, Bluooo!" Blue was gone. He probably flogged the wrong person in south Lubbock and came to a bad end.

Ma's granddaughter Katy also loves birds. She once had a pair of finches. I made for her Christmas present that year a tall bamboo cage from a Japanese kit. The instructions were badly translated. "Put (A) thin sticks up, (B) thick sticks cross. Be careful put end pieces where belong." That was about it and the cage was three graduated stories high, with a *cupola*. A week of my life was spent on that cage.

The finches were Zebra finches. He was striped gray and white with a rose-colored collar. Katy named them Leroy and Rose. Rose was white, as a bride should be. Tiny birds, they were cute in that cage. At least I thought so, until they were left in my care for an extended visit. Katy had bought a little nest for the cage, and I found eggs in it. "Oh great," I thought, "maybe we'll have some babies when Katy comes home."

She had left a long list of things to do for the birds, the last one underlined: *Speak softly to the birds.*

Well, I did speak softly to the birds, until I noticed that Rose not only was not sitting on the eggs, but she looked peculiar. Her feathers on her left side were all ruffled up and she had a bare spot, bereft of feathers, on her neck. Leroy was abusive. I caught him in the act. He was methodically plucking her feathers out in rows. I began to speak harshly to him and finally found a weapon, a chopstick, fitting for the Japanese cage. I would whack him hard across his back when I found him at it. To no avail. When Katy came home, poor Rose was as naked as a jaybird. I think she died of pneumonia. Two more brides met the same fate. As soon as they laid their eggs, they were plucked bare. Not like Duchamp's bride, the bride stripped bare by the bachelors, but the brides stripped bare by the bridegroom.

When the third bride died of exposure, we had all moved to Austin and Katy lived in a little house in Tarrytown. On piers, the house was five feet or so off the ground at the rear. One morning she found evidence that a rat had been in her house. She discovered, too late, that it came up through the dryer outlet under the house. The next day, more signs of the rat. The third morning, she found a hole in Leroy's cage, where he had lived all alone. There were feathers all about and Leroy and the rat were gone. I laughed out loud. Leroy was rotten to the core.

But the saddest bird I've ever known was Katy's mockingbird. Katy had an art gallery and studio, just above Buffalo Bayou on Sandman in Houston. She was working there one day when she saw a cat after a baby mockingbird. She rushed out and saved her. Or so she thought. She assumed the new baby, barely sprouting feathers, mouth wide open, was a girl. Katy called bird rescuers and learned what to feed her, little pellets of ground meat mixed with baby cereal and water from a medicine dropper. She named her Maria for Maria Callas, her favorite opera star. Maria the mockingbird never sang.

I always thought that the male mockingbird sang all night to attract a female. Not so, both males and females sing. And I thought that their songs were stolen. Only ten percent is mimicry, the rest their own repertoire. They simply have an overwhelming urge to sing. Isn't that grand?

Maria, kept in a little cage and fed constantly, began to look like a real mockingbird. She wasn't. We let her fly free on our screened back porch and she learned to eat her own food and water from a bowl. She graduated to the backyard, where Katy tried to teach her to hunt pill bugs. Maria did not want to hunt pill bugs. She only ate one if offered on the palm of a hand. She was then left outside all day. When Katy came in from work, she would stand in the backyard, hold up her forefinger, and call, "Maria!" Maria would instantly land on the finger. Sometimes Katy wouldn't call her name, but would wait. No matter. Maria would land on her head and Katy would come in with that bird on her head, looking like a younger version of my mother with her pet crow riding her head, had the crow been small, gray, and hungry.

And then it was time to go to Galveston on vacation. We debated whether to take the bird in her cage, as we had often done on weekends, or to leave her free. My husband said, "Oh, leave her! She will make it; she's been out nearly a month." Oh? Paul had to come back to town after a week for some business. As he turned into the driveway he met Maria, racing down the drive on the ground, mouth open, screaming bloody murder. He left his car at the foot of the drive, where she attached herself to his shoulder and went in with him. He gave her part of his supper, cheese and salami. Paul returned to Galveston, leaving her outside with a bowl of cheese and salami.

The next week, a business friend of Paul's on his way home from work rang our doorbell. Maria was instantly on his shoulder, startling and even frightening him. He said he had never had a wild bird on his shoulder and that he spent the worst forty-five minutes of his life trying to get it off. He tried to leave her. She wanted to go with him. He kept ripping her off his shoulder, fraying his suit. He put her on the grass and ran for his car, over and over, finally in panic. Each time, Maria was firmly attached before he was behind the wheel.

He wondered what our neighbors must think to see a grown man in a business suit, fighting, throwing, chasing, and even cursing a mockingbird. At last, he threw her between the azaleas and the house. He was gone before she could extricate herself. The friend, home late, was met at the door by his wife, who stared at his ruined coat, his pale face, and the wild look still in his eyes. "Don't ask!" he said.

We came home. Didn't see Maria. Well, we said, she must have made it. I had an art studio in the little servant's quarters over the garage. I put, as usual and just in case, some of her food and water on the rail of the landing. I stepped out there in a day or so, just to stare around. There, at my eye level, was the mockingbird on a telephone wire. Like Leonard Cohen's bird on a wire, like his drunk in a midnight choir. Our bird never sang, but she tried in her way to be free.

She didn't come down to eat, she just sat on that wire, her eyes as big as marbles. When I looked into those pale, pitiful eyes, I almost cried. She was a bone, her feathers gone in spots, and she had only two tail feathers, one hanging limply down and one askew. Could there be anything more mournful on the face of this earth than a dying mockingbird?

Do you hear that old dove?

THE COLLECTORS

I love solitude. I have never understood how my mother, my sister, and my daughter could do without it. There's an old song that sometimes hovers around in my brain and just drives me crazy. "Good night, Irene. Good night, Irene. I'll see you in my dreams." When I hear it, I picture a long line of beaus in top hats singing to a beautiful woman. And I see my old sister Bob when she was a beautiful girl with her long line of beaus, though not in top hats. And sometimes in my dreams I see my daughter Katy, who is also beautiful and had a long line of beaus, though by then they were called *boy friends*. A pity. I knew that Katy had inherited the "collector" gene. She and Bob are so alike, so beautiful and so crazy.

Their looks have nothing to do with it. They exude a mad sweetness, an aura that attracts people, both male and female. In their young days, many males gathered about. And so they began their lifelong collection, not of butterflies, but of people, never knowing solitude and never missing it. There is another line from that old song I hear over and over when Katy and Bob are both on my mind. "Sometimes I live in the country and sometimes I live in town. Sometimes I take a great notion to jump in the river and drown."

They inherited the collector gene from my mother. When she was old, she speculated about how much better her life would have been had she married this one or that one or the other. Collecting people, the odder the better, she was never alone. When she had to take in boarders, she loved it. She took them in and kept them forever. She spent all of her life with her family, except for me. She cried all day on my wedding day, though I was twenty-four. It was not that I was marrying, but leaving.

My daughter Leslie has the gene and the beauty, but with it she inherited, from her father and his mother, her cheekbones and a shy gene of reserve and introversion. Having a counterbalance for the zany gene, she pulled people in the front door with one hand and pushed them out the back with the other. Her divided heart made her a poet. (I stole "divided heart" from one of her poems.)

I knew that Katy had the gene early on, when I found a bouquet of wilted flowers scattered around our front door early one morning. I learned that a little boy had stolen his mother's flowers and thrown them against our door for Katy. I said to myself, "Uh-oh."

I said Uh-oh because I had a flashback. I saw myself at fourteen, sitting on the front porch of a rented house during the Depression. We had lost our old white house and were in our second rented one. But we still had a porch. Sitting there with me and my mother were two couples who had been our boarders in the old white house. They had come through Memphis and stopped off for some time with us. While we were sitting there at sundown, reminiscing, a handsome boy arrived dressed in his best for his date with Bob. She came out looking like the Queen of Memphis, which she was, and left with the boy.

Soon another boy arrived. "Well," Ma said. "Come in and sit with us." "No," he said, "I have a date with Bobby." My poor mother said that oh she was very sorry, but Bob had already gone out. He left, dejected. And then there came a third young man, full of hope. The boarders collapsed in their chairs, slapping their knees and laughing. Ma and I didn't laugh all that much. We were used to it. Bob could never say no.

My mother said Bob had this strange attraction for people because she was born with a caul. A caul is the membrane that surrounds a fetus. Sometimes a portion of it covers a baby's head at birth. It was considered a sign of good luck. Ma thought it had other powers, an omen of greatness, giving the baby something that ordinary people don't have. Bob was a smart girl and could have done well in school, but she was always looking for fun. And my mother was always looking for Bob.

Bob thought Ma was psychic. She was, but she also knew Bob's mind, having the same gene. Bob would go over the river into Oklahoma with a car full of kids to drink beer. She would throw up on the way home and get up the next morning, pale and sick. She could never understand how Ma knew where she had been. She wasn't as smart as we thought.

She was always in trouble in high school. She was a cheerleader, voted most popular, most beautiful, and all of those things. But she had too many friends and felt obligated to entertain them. One morning she was picking up absentee slips. She opened the door to the biology class, taught by the principal. She stuck her head in and not seeing him, asked, "Where is old man Gore? Where is the old goat?" The old goat rose up from behind a counter. This kind of thing did her no good in high school, but she was famous for it.

My mother never heard of "parent participation." Bob played hooky with her friends in high school. Ma was supposed to have a visit with the principal before Bob could go back to class. She refused to go. "Why should

I have to quit my work, walk to school and see Mr. Gore? *I* didn't play hooky." The other truants were in school the next day. Bob sat crying in Mr. Gore's office for days. Finally he lost control and took her to Ma's kitchen for the conference. Bob never played hooky again. Principals no longer go to kitchens.

Once Ma and I, walking to the north part of town to see my Aunt Gussie, stopped by the school looking for Bob. She hadn't come home that day. We found her on a ladder; she was painting the band house. The little building was covered in graffiti: "Down with Supt. Davis." The new superintendent had fired the much-loved coach, Chesty Walker. The students walked out of school and also painted those words all over the new stadium. Bob and her cohorts spent afternoons for weeks repainting the band house and the stadium. She was blamed for those giant black words because, Mr. Gore told Ma, had she not walked out to do it, no one else would have. She had that kind of power. Whether from the caul or not, I don't know.

My mother's hair stayed black until she was nearly seventy. I'll never understand it. Mine began to gray in my forties when Katy was only thirteen, the night Ed Owen called to tell us that she was in jail. Katy had gone to spend the night with her friend Kay Owen just around the block. Katy and Kay had slipped out of the house at two in the morning to meet a boy and go for a late, very late, night walk. The boy was stuck on Katy and he was, or so my husband thought, eccentric, if not mad. Paul had forbidden Katy to have anything at all to do with him. This was in the Houston suburb of Meyerland in the sixties. Times were strange.

The police, answering a call about a loud party and a fight, had seen this strange threesome, picked them up, and taken them "downtown." Kay, who had scoliosis, was wearing a neck brace that reached to her waist, making her somewhat immobile. The police, helping her into the patrol car, slammed the door on her thumb, causing her to cry and sob all the way downtown. I don't think Katy ever cried. I am afraid she found it rather exciting.

My Leslie, that same night, was very ill with mono-nucleosis. Her fever was one hundred and five de-grees and I was wide awake, listening for her, when the phone rang about four. I heard my husband say, "WHAT, WANDERING THE STREETS?" I thought Leslie had wandered out in her delirium. I sprang out of bed, aging ten years, and was pleased to learn that it was only Katy in jail. The next day Paul gave her three whacks with his old fraternity paddle. Katy said he beat the stuffing out of her, but I heard the punish-ment. He gave her three whacks. It did her no harm, and it helped her father a lot.

A while back I found some pages on which Katy had written a hundred times in perfect handwriting, "I will keep my parents informed of where I am at all times." When she was grown her writing deteriorated. Today it looks just like Ma's, all squiggles and dashes. I think Ma's spirit must have come to Katy, saying, "Pay 'em no mind."

Katy adopted people. In high school, she adopted a boy named Bun. He was fourteen and brilliant. He played the viola and could draw and write. He made and illustrated wonderful miniature books. Katy brought Bun home every day after school. His mother couldn't handle him and had sent him to Houston to live with his homosexual brother. His brother, I think, was a decorator and worked all the time. Bun was lonesome. Katy would go out on dates, leaving him to me. Bun would slash up my new Formica counters making sandwiches, and then roll around on my oriental rug with a Coke, eating popcorn and watching TV. I sat up with him until Katy took him home. He said he was afraid to ride the bus, but he was waiting for Katy, of course. I wonder where Bun is.

Bob also adopted people. Among the missionaries and alcoholics were many hair stylists. She loved having her hair done; it was a necessity for her. She had known her first hair stylist, however, since he was a child and she loved him. She often took him in, the last time in his forties, trying to "save" him from his homosexuality and drugs. She didn't save him. The drugs got him, but some of the best years of his life were spent in her house.

One day at the beauty salon, her stylist, Carmen, was crying. She was being evicted and had no money and no place to go. Of course, Bob brought her home. Carmen was Puerto Rican and had grown up in Harlem. She was wild. How she got to Lubbock, I don't know, but Bob kept her close. She finally married a football player, moved away, and had a little boy. I wonder where she is.

And then there was Alicia, a gorgeous Mexican girl from San Antonio. She had been adopted young by a woman who used her as a maid. She spoke good English, but couldn't read it. She had to be taken everywhere. She couldn't read street signs and was always lost in Lubbock. She married an Air Force pilot and moved to Spain. She wrote to Bob for years, in Spanish. I wonder where she is.

When Katy was a new mother, she adopted two deaf boys, Jimmy Turner and his roommate, Bob. They lived in the apartment above hers in Clarksville. Dancers and acrobats, they were in Austin to dance with the Spectrum American Deaf Dance Company. Late at night above Katy's head, they noisily shoved the furniture to the walls and their feet pounded the floor to an African beat for hours. And the strangest thing, while they were dancing, tumbling, and doing somersaults, they laughed aloud. They lived in silence, but their thumping and bumping and pounding of feet was punctuated with loud laughter. They couldn't speak or hear, but they could laugh.

They were often in Katy's house, especially at suppertime. They had no phone, of course. Katy learned sign language so she could speak to them, take their calls, and interpret. She is still good at it. Bob, a tall, handsome white boy, went home to Florida. Jimmy, a beautiful, muscular black man in dreadlocks, a wonderful dancer, still dances in Austin. And laughs.

She also collected three artists, all male, when her baby was still small. They hung around her house, watching her paint, just to be near her. They were sweet boys, one Pakistani, one Iranian, and one a Houston boy. No longer boys, they are gone from Austin now. Katy still loves them. And so do I.

She collects people of diverse backgrounds. Two of her best friends are English girls. And there is Mirna Fiorini, a teenager she met on the street in Rome when Katy was a teenager herself. She saw Mirna again at college age. That time, Mirna's mother fed Katy green tomatoes, saved for special occasions. I knew Mirna myself and had a memorable lunch with her on the Via Veneto in a famous sidewalk cafe. I still think of Mirna. I hope she has a happy life.

And just this spring there was Sasha, from a village in the Czech Republic. My granddaughter, Carrie, brought Sasha home with her from Amsterdam. Sasha was to live in Houston while she studied English. She was unhappy there, so, of course, Katy took her in, finding her a tutor, helping her with her English, and feeding and entertaining her as best she could. Sasha went home crying, wanting to stay with Katy forever.

Katy's first husband was a musician. Mexican American, he was the third generation in Texas, son of a chemical engineer who went to Rice University. David was a poet and songwriter. Oh, how he could play the guitar. He became a lawyer, but he remained a songwriter. One of my favorite train songs is his. It says, "She hits you like a train and then she goes." Her second husband was a big Iowa farm boy, different enough. He was a carpenter, built houses, but he is about to become a clinical psychologist. No wonder. And then, for a while, she lived with a Peruvian artist. Her daughter's first real beau was Belgian, from Brussels. Stranger still, her second love is an opera singer, a tenor, from Lufkin, Texas. I had prayed that the gene would skip a generation.

Katy's aura drew in wildlife as well as people. She had many birds and small animals, various species of rats, hamsters, kangaroo rats (the jumping kind), and others. She named all of the rodents Otis. She had a mockingbird, but that is another story.

She left her dog, Alice, to me when she went to college. Alice, named for Alice B. Toklas, became my dog. I loved her, took care of her, and she loved me. But the minute Katy walked in the front door, Alice abandoned me and stuck to her like glue. If I just raised my voice when speaking to Katy, Alice growled menacingly, wanting to bite me. Once I playfully slapped Katy on the seat when she was asleep on the couch. When I raised my arm, Alice was dangling there, her jaws clamped around my wrist. She was an ingrate, but she couldn't help it. She loved Katy best.

My mother loved birds, but her gene collected dogs and cats, though she denied it and pretended to hate them, threatening and warning them to keep their distance. They didn't. All of our pets loved her best. She walked through the house, a sea of animals following in her wake. Her last days were spent with her grandson's big German shepherd, Missy. Missy came early every morning for coffee. One big paw on Ma's screen door and she was in. They sat with their coffee—Ma with her cup, Missy's in a large bowl with sugar and cream—smiling at one another. Later, when Ma was nearly ninety, Missy came one morning and could not lift her paw to the screen. She had an incurable disease. Missy took a lick of her coffee and went into the garage. This woman, who hated pets, made a soft bed for the big dog, petting and speaking softly to her all day as she was dying.

One day when Katy was working at her easel on Indian Trail in Austin, she felt a strange sensation at her foot. An old, gray Chihuahua was wrapped around her ankle, shivering and looking up at her with soulful eyes. Katy consoled that old dog until late in the afternoon, when she took it out and found a friend, an *anciano*, an ancient Mexican man who lived next door. The dog was his visitor. An *anciano* in Tarrytown was odd enough, but the Chihuahua was odder. Her name was Daisy and she came from Pflugerville. The old man couldn't imagine how she got out and Katy couldn't imagine how she got in. But I know.

Bob, though, was missing a bit of DNA from her gene. She really didn't care for animals, nor they for her. It was odd. Her gene drew in only the human species. One night on Twenty-second Street in Lubbock, Bob had gone to bed early. She had been ill and she was leaving town early in the morning, maybe to come to my house. Alicia was in her room next to Bob's, doing her nails and talking, as usual, with her heavy accent ninety miles a minute to nobody in particular. Bob's husband, Jerry, was in the front bedroom telling his made-up tales about a jackrabbit named Squimpsy to a bed full of grandchildren. They were laughing and shrieking. In bed with Bob was Susie, an opera singer from Pampa. A great soprano, she also was in bed early, because she was singing the next day. The phone rang at nine. A friend was visiting an old woman in a rest home. The old woman was depressed, crying, and the friend wanted to bring her to Bob for cheering up. Of course.

The old lady was established in a rocking chair at the foot of the bed. Bob sat up, began to ask her questions, to tease her, and to tell her funny stories. The old lady began to smile and to tell her own tales, laughing and having a wonderful time. Finally, the friend took the old woman on her walker, chuckling and giggling, back to her lonely room.

It was midnight. Bob fell back on her pillows, exhausted. The soprano, whose eyes had been shut tight during this whole scene, opened one of them. She asked, in her beautiful voice, "Is this a zoo, or what?!"

A DISH AND A BOWL

There is a bullet hole in my old majolica dish. More than a hundred years old, it is a small platter shaped like a leaf. The glaze is worn off the acorns scattered over it. A shiny green, shading into umber at the edges, it is still beautiful. It belonged to my grandmother, Augusta Jane McDaniel, born the fourth child of John and Jane McKinley McDaniel on June 14, 1863, in Limestone County. My mother was the fourth child of Augusta Jane, who died in childbirth with her ninth. The dish and her dough bowl are the only things my mother ever had of hers. I have them both.

I can't remember when Ma didn't have the dish. Maybe it was given to her when she married, but knowing her, I suspect she took it when her mother died. My grandmother didn't have many nice things in that poor little house in Eutaw, where they all lived for a time. Eutaw is gone now, nothing left but ruins of some old chimneys and a historical marker. When my grandmother died, her household was broken up and the children were taken by her sister, Ophelia, and her husband, Zachary. They raised the new baby and the little ones to adulthood, helping the older ones as best they could. They were saints. They had no children of their own, but they raised thirteen orphans, some not even kin. We called them Auntie and Uncle. They were full of boundless love. I didn't know my grandparents, but I never felt sorry for myself, because I had Auntie and Uncle.

Ma resented her father after her mother died, often referring to him as "that old rascal." "That old rascal," she said, "took up with women and gave away my mother's things." Augusta had a lovely, handmade wooden bed, which Ma coveted. Once, years and years later, when she was visiting her sisters in Kosse, they went into the country to see a very old woman. Sitting in the parlor, my mother could see into a bedroom. There was her mother's bed. "That old rascal," she thought.

Her father corrected her English, singling her out from the other children, whom he didn't correct. I know they got the message; she was his example. He said she knew better. Once at supper she told someone to "take and putt" this in the kitchen (not *put*, but *putt*). He reached over and popped her on the cheek. "Say, take this to the kitchen," he said. Or if she said, "We all seen it," he would pop her one and say "we saw." She did speak pretty good English for a country girl and she should have been grateful, but she hated him for it. And for her mother's bed.

The bullet hole in the majolica dish was not made in Limestone County, but down on Seventh Street in Memphis in the Kestersons' living room. Their small child, Bill George, shot the hole in it with his twenty-two rifle. His mother, Susy, had borrowed the dish to display with some old things for the Old Settlers' Reunion. Bill George also shot a hole in a leaded glass pane by our front door. His rifle was confiscated after that. Bill George grew up to be the deputy sheriff in Hall County.

He was a cute little kid when he wasn't armed. He stuttered. His mother asked him one day what he wanted to do. "Go over to K-k-k-kate's and j-jump on the beds," he said. Ma allowed bed-jumping. On our sleeping porch we had three double beds and we bounced from bed to bed, laughing and shouting. No trampoline could have been more fun. A friend of Ma's, on hearing us and seeing her unperturbed, finally could stand it no longer and asked, "Do you not hear those children jumping on your beds?" "I do," my mother replied.

My grandmother's big bowl, round and crude, was made from a tree in Eutaw. Gussie, as she was called, made her bread in it. Ma never made bread in it. She brought it home from Kosse once after visiting her sisters and brothers. I think Aunt Sister gave it to her. My sister Loisie scrubbed off a hundred years of flour and refinished it. I wish she hadn't, but it looks pretty on my kitchen counter and has not one crack in it. Auntie also had a bowl made from that same old tree. It is a rectangle. My mother found it once in Kosse in a storage shed, maybe behind Aunt Sister's house. She said she hugged that bowl and cried. She stole it, hid it in her suitcase and brought it home. My sister Bob has it.

I call mine my Eutaw bowl. My grandmother's grand-mother came in a wagon train and made that place. Her name was Nancy Wallace McKinley and she was a Cherokee. My mother told me that some of her female cousins from Waco had traced the McKinleys back to Nancy Wallace and found that she was an Indian. Horrified, they hid away their family tree under a bed. They were ashamed of their Indian blood. Their brother years later did it again and I have a nice book, *The McKinley Clan,* all of us included clear back to Nancy, with a picture of her, but still no mention of her heritage.

I know that she was a full-blooded Cherokee because my mother told me. Her mother told her and her grandmother told her mother. That grandmother was the daughter of Nancy, the Cherokee. I believe them and I treasure every drop of her blood.

I know that Nancy named the town of Eutaw. My Houston cousin, Spencer Lowery, grew up in Kosse. He knows all about Limestone County and he says that Eutaw is a Cherokee word. I haven't been able to find out what it means. I hope it means *sacred ground,* for Eutaw is sacred ground to me.

Nancy's name is not on the historical marker east of Kosse on Highway 7. Charles Carson McKinley's and his brother's names are there, but not the names of their wives. It is the same with other markers in Texas, as if the fathers came alone. Under the ruins of those old chimneys in Eutaw and other places, I see the mothers cooking over their fires in the rock fireplaces and I see them working like dogs to get there in their wagons and to make all of the little towns, but their names have been left off the markers. Such a pity.

Why is it that these old things that we keep and love stir us up so? Someday they will all be thrown out or sold in a garage sale, if they still have garages, by children who don't know why their mothers saved them. They will be gone as all old things must go.

When I put my fruit in my grandmother's bowl, I feel her presence and can see her bread rising. When I contemplate her majolica dish, I feel an awful sadness that I never knew her. I also see my mother and remember what a good mother she was. And sometimes just a glance at the old dish, with its bullet hole, gives me a terrible urge to jump on beds.

A WIDENING

Leon Hale, a great Texas writer and columnist, once challenged his readers to come up with the most remarkable or significant event in their lives. I started trying to find mine. My wedding day? I thought so at the time. As a painter, I won many awards long ago. Each time I won, I thought nothing better would ever happen. Wrong, as it turned out. It didn't amount to much. I was acquired by a museum. "This is the ulti-mate," I thought. "What could top it?" In the long run, it made no difference.

When I was a poor child in West Texas, I submitted a drawing for the golden anniversary monument that stands today on the courthouse square in Hall County. There was a grand ceremony down on the square and

I won the twenty-five dollar award. Never having owned that much money, I thought, "This is it!" But, no. It was only money. I still smile when I see my drawing chiseled into that old monument. My name isn't even on it.

And so, I dredged on into my past, looking for my most remarkable event. I found it. I had it three times. It came with my babies. It didn't happen on the days of their births, though they were grand enough.

There is a time when a baby is still an immigrant, hasn't learned the language, doesn't know who or where he is, around two months, when his comic little face begins to show true emotion, his eyes focus, and he finds his voice. Happy babies begin to coo their funny little baby sounds, sort of a singing. Or whistling, in my granddaughter's case. A strange child, she found her whistle when she found her voice. Some mornings, instead of cooing, she would whistle a little baby song.

One lucky morning, usually early, you will hear your baby and go. On that day, a happy baby will be cooing and chortling away when you come. At that magic moment, your baby will pause, and in silence, will look at you with a strange and mysterious widening of the eyes, an amazed look of the purest happiness you will ever see. I can't find a word for the look. *Widen* is the only one that comes to mind. It is a look of pure dee love. As if they suddenly realize that this is a grand place they have come to and they know who you are. At that moment, your life widens and *you* know who you are. You are a mother and will be one forever.

I've never had a problem with this concept of forever, but my mother thought that once a mother, always a mother, was a great burden. "Why is it," she asked me once, "that you aggravate me more at twenty-four than you did when you were four?" (I aggravated her at twenty-four because I was marrying too young.) And she often told us that if we went to the ends of the earth, we would never escape, that she would find us even if she was a hundred. She would be a hundred and ten now and I still feel her lurking around.

That morning when she saw our eyes widen put us in her clutches, never to escape. And the pity of it, today, the look is often lost on sitters and strangers in daycare, or worse. All who have babies must see it. I'm sure it comes to fathers, though I have never heard one mention it. I was blessed with it three times, twice with my daughters and a third glorious time with my granddaughter. She has the biggest and most beautiful eyes that anyone could be fortunate enough to be born with. My daughter Leslie came into this world with knowing eyes, as bright and black as a polecat's and as wise as an old woman's. Katy came with amber, laughing eyes, ready to make fun of it all.

When your babies are growing up, they quit cooing and chortling. There are down times, when their wicked eyes will look at you with the wrong kind of knowledge and their mouths will make ugly sounds. But that pure loving baby look is safe in your soul. It may be all downhill from there, or uphill as my mother would say. She referred to the teen years as Fool's Hill. "Oh, he will be all right," she would say of some kid in a barrel of trouble, "when he makes it up Fool's Hill."

It is a miracle, but my three finally made it up Fool's Hill and came out on the high plain. Once in a while when I look at them, I feel that same old surge of amazed love and happiness and my eyes widen in a look of wild surmise, like old Cortez, silent upon his peak in Darien.

MOTHERS AND BABIES

The first new baby I ever knew was my nephew Georgie. I knew him too well. I knew everything that went in his upper end and everything that came out the lower end and how to clean him up after this process. I knew what happened to those cloth diapers, so lovingly collected before his birth. They were dunked in the commode, boiled in my Ma's old black pot, and hung in the sun, every single day. I knew how to get mucus and dried mucus (boogers) out of his nose with a Q-Tip. I knew how to cut his finger-nails without cutting off his tiny fingers, so he wouldn't scratch his face and eyes.

Oh, I knew more than I ever wanted to know about Georgie and I was just an innocent child myself when he was born in the front bedroom of our old white house down on Seventh Street in Memphis, Texas, in 1936. His mother, my oldest sister, Loisie, though she lived in Clarendon only thirty miles away, came home three months before he was born to be with her mother and near Dr. O.R. Goodall, one of the best doctors who ever lived in Hall County. Unfortunately for my mother, Georgie came on a Saturday. My mother sent my brother, John, and me to the movies at ten o'clock in the morning. Unusual enough, but she also gave us twenty cents extra to buy a hamburger, Coke, and popcorn. We didn't question our good luck; we were too dumb to wonder why. "Hang around the square awhile," she said. "Eat your lunch and go to the movie. Do not come home until you've seen it twice." We always saw it twice and obeyed until one-thirty, when someone came down the aisle, announcing in a loud voice, "Lois has had the baby. It's a boy!" We jumped up, all the Seventh Street kids, and we ran, ten or twelve of us, across the square to Main Street, down Seventh and into the house. My mother was extremely aggravated with us, but Dr. Goodall let us see the baby. I was shocked at the sight of him, thirty minutes old, red, pointed head, half-washed. "Will he look that way forever?" I wondered. He didn't. In a week, he was handsome and, sixty years later, still is.

By the time his sister Mary Lynn was born, they had moved to Lubbock, but Lois still came home for her three months with her mother and her doctor. She was the world's worst mamma's baby until she died. The Depression had taken our white house and we lived in a rented brown one across the street. Mary (called Titta) came at four-thirty in the morning. Dr. Goodall brought her into the living room, which was full of neighbors and friends drinking coffee and waiting. She was passed around the room like a gift at a shower. She was prettier than Georgie and still is. Lois had two more, Kay and Karen (Toopey and Stinky), but they were born in hospitals and their births weren't near so much fun. Hospitals frown on crowds of dirty kids, oohing and aahing and playing with the baby's fingers.

My sister Lois was the ultimate mother. Only twelve when I was born, she mothered John and me. Her name for John was Hound. Well, he did bawl a lot, howling, she called it, hence the Hound. She gave us cod liver oil every morning, cleaned our ears and faces daily, and once a week, if Ma didn't, she put us in the tub, soaped our hair, and poured buckets of water over our heads, with much screaming and howling. She loved it.

And one day, when she was two blocks west of home, at the house of her best friend, Joan Estes, she saw a herd of cattle coming down that street on their way to the railroad. When she had left home, John and I were playing in the ditch. She ran in front of the herd, crying and calling our names the two blocks home, where Ma ran out, grabbed her, and dragged her to safety. "Child," Ma asked, "do you think these children don't have enough sense to come in out of a herd of cattle? Had you stampeded those cows, they would have killed you." John and I went to the front porch the minute we heard the cattle and the cowboys. From a mile away we could hear their lowing and bawling and shouting and hooting. We were accustomed to cattle drives on our side street and we knew where the best seats were for the grand performance. Lord, what I would give to see it just one more time.

Loisie worshipped babies, never happier than when she was bathing or feeding one. She raised hers and most of her grandchildren. She was a strange girl. She loved cooking and cleaning, nursing the sick and wiping babies' rear ends. She was always giving, never needing. She was at my house when my only grand-child was born in Houston. Loisie was being treated at M.D. Anderson Hospital and was dying. She had lost her right breast to a rare cancer when my granddaughter, Carrie, was born. Lois insisted on giving Carrie her first bath. Her right arm useless, she flopped Carrie expertly around on her lap with her left, scrubbing, laughing, and cooing. She had a lot of fun when she was dying, because she had a new baby to play with, a wonderful coincidence.

I've never known another woman like her. It was like having two mothers, because she came home every third weekend after she married, unless I was at her house. I was the baby, the only one free to go, so she took me along. She could not be without us. I spent summer weeks in Altus, Oklahoma, or Portales, New Mexico, and even six weeks in Dallas, where I saw Roosevelt in the 1936 Centennial Parade. I threw up on the trolley going home to Oak Cliff.

But the summer afternoons burned in my memory were in Portales. We lived in a little adobe house, across the street from the maternity ward of the Portales Hospital. By noon the house was too hot to live in, so Loisie would bring out a big quilt, spread it under the tree, and bring a grand lunch on a tray. Georgie, two years old, Loisie, five months along with his sister, and I would eat that lunch, and then take a nap on our quilt, while, from across the street, we could hear moans and groans and screams. Lois would murmur to me as she drifted to sleep and I lay there with big eyes, "Don't pay any attention, they're just being silly, it doesn't hurt that much."

Though she once lived in Wyoming, she never went more than a month or two without seeing her mother and she died the year after Ma's death, still grieving. A friend told her to stop mourning, that her mother was ninety; it was time for her to go. "I don't care," Lois replied. "I'm going over to Memphis and dig her up." Her sense of humor saved her; she knew she was ridiculous. Oh, she played golf, bridge, joined study clubs and such, but her heart was home with her babies and she watched the clock until she could get back there. She was the only woman I ever knew who cared only for family, hearth, and home.

My first baby, Leslie, was born in Houston. I lived in a duplex on Vassar, a short street that is right on the Southwest Freeway today. At that time, in 1952, there was a park where the freeway is, with a swimming pool. I swam in it every day and walked up Dunlavy to Richmond where I bought my groceries in the Weingartens. When I was carrying Leslie the walk was my daily exercise. I don't suppose you could cross the freeway now on foot. But I still love the memory of that walk through the neighborhood with its beautiful trees to the old store.

Leslie, I thought, of course, the prettiest baby ever born. She *was* unusual. She had the brightest, shining eyes. They were never vague as a new baby's eyes can be. One morning when she was three months old, she was in her bed by the window, which opened onto the driveway. I was talking to her and she was cooing back at me when an old woman who lived next door came across the driveway and looked in. I didn't know her, except to speak, but I thought she was old. She may have been sixty, old to me at the time. "She is a pretty baby," she said, and spoke softly to Les through the window. Les gurgled back. Then she looked at me and in a bitter voice said,

"Love her while you can, for when she is grown, she will break your heart." Then she turned and walked away. It was like being visited by Sleeping Beauty's evil fairy, making her wicked wish. I was depressed for a while, but I shrugged it off. "We have no spindles now," I thought.

The neighbor had a lovely daughter, a pretty, delicate girl with long red hair. I had seen her come and go from school, but she left home and, I learned from neighbors, she was a lesbian. Later, I saw the daughter come home in a cab. She left it waiting. Her hair was cut short and she wore a man's suit, but she was still pretty. After that, I heard that she had been arrested on drug charges. I wonder which was the spindle that pricked the daughter's finger and broke the mother's heart. Was it the daughter's homosexuality? Back then, it could have been. Or were drugs the spindle? Or did they, like Sleeping Beauty and the king and queen, wake up one day and live happily ever after?

Leslie never broke my heart, but she once gave it a whack. It takes more than a whack to break a heart. She ran off and married a boy she couldn't live with. I knew the minute I saw him that we were in trouble. He had grand dark eyes, a deep, persuasive preacher's voice, and black curly hair that stood six inches high. Les, a teenage hippie, was in her first year at college. She brought him home for Christmas. After Christmas, they ran off to Amarillo and were married. Eighteen, she was old enough. Lois had done the same at eighteen and she lived a long and happy married life. Leslie's elopement would have been harder on me but for the way that she did it. After the shock and the crying I found it funny, though I hid that fact from her daddy, as he was so distraught. She took off on a Greyhound bus, her hair long and parted in the middle, wearing wire-frame glasses, no make-up, and a long, olive-drab cape from army surplus, with a cat in a box tucked under her arm.

She disappeared for two weeks, two bad weeks. I was more worried about her dropping out of school than I was about her. I knew she could take care of herself, but I thought to be without an education would be her spindle as she was a child who loved learning. I needn't have worried. She not only went back to school, but stayed and stayed through three degrees. She did start up those fatal steps, but turned back before she reached the room at the top of the tower.

The strangest baby I ever knew was Hugo. Hugo was a gorilla that had been orphaned in Africa and adopted by his missionary parents. They brought him home to live with them on Mandell, near Richmond. I really didn't know Hugo well, but became acquainted with him at Weingartens. When I first saw him, in his diaper, held against his mother Annie's chest, his little arms wrapped around her neck, his shining black eyes peering over her shoulder, he made me forget what I had come to the grocery store for. After a while, Hugo's mother refused to answer questions or talk about him. She had to, or else she would have bought food surrounded by a mob. I finally was able to quit staring at him. After all, he was just another baby. We moved out off South Main and I never saw Hugo again, but I read in the paper that they had given him to the zoo when he grew too big to handle. Annie visited him every day until he got the flu. She brought him home and built a big cage with bars opening onto her living room. He lived there until he died, weighing five hundred pounds. At least Annie never had to worry about him being out late at night. The neighbors may have.

When I still lived on Vassar, my niece Penny came from Lubbock to see me. She was four. I took her to the store and there was Hugo. She looked at that furry baby and stood stock-still, her big eyes got bigger, and her Lubbock mouth dropped open. Finally she asked, "Whut kind of a baby is tha-et?"

I dragged her away, telling her I would explain about Hugo at home. But, durn, when we left the store, there on the sidewalk was an organ grinder with his monkey. Now Penny knew about monkeys, but had never seen one dancing about in a little suit with his hat in his hand. "Is tha-et monkey a little ki-ed?" she asked as I hurried her home. "I will explain," I told her, and I did explain, over and over and over about the ape and the monkey. Long after bedtime, she would call out, "Now, whut?" There were no apes or monkeys in Lubbock then and probably none now.

We were all babies once and it may be the one true thing we have in common. We are all so different from one another, thank the Lord. With any luck, our folks loved us and didn't worry about what we would become. My friend Dorothy Robertson (from Hull-Daisetta), when her first was born, asked her doctor-brother, "Bubba, how old must a baby be before you know it has good sense?" "Sister," Bubba replied, "sometimes you can tell by the time it is thirty-five."

After all, no one, not even a bad fairy, can predict how the beautiful baby will turn out. Could Annie have dreamed, when she chose not to abandon her sweet Hugo in Africa, that he would grow to be untouchable, a huge ape swinging on a rope and screaming around in a concrete cage in her living room? It wouldn't have mattered; she loved him until he died. How about Stewart Little's mother? A fictional mother, but real to Les, Katy, and me. Her second son, the ultimate odd baby, was obviously different when he was just a few days old. He was not only looking like a mouse, but was acting like one. He began to wear a little gray hat and carry a small cane. And, I suppose, his tail was evident by then. It made no difference to his mother; she loved him and my babies loved him when I read his story to them over and over and over. Who could not love Stewart Little, tail and all? And then there was the Duchess, who was abusing her baby when Alice rescued him, only to find the baby turning into a pig in her arms. It took a lot to discourage Alice, as we know. Alice, the optimist, let the baby go into the woods, telling herself it would have been a dreadfully ugly child, but it *was* a handsome pig.

My mother used to say that all of her babies and grandbabies were pretty because she preferred pretty, and God knew her too well to take a chance with ugly. Oh, I don't know about John and me. There are no baby pictures of us. I like to blame that on the Depression. But, so far, in her family, I have known three generations of babies—all of them beautiful. So far, it's hard to predict how they will turn out, though many are past thirty-five and the bedroom-born ones are sixty or more. But, so far, none have grown snouts, long tails, worn little gray hats, carried tiny canes, or swung on ropes in concrete cages.

So far.

SOUVENIR

It's old and faded, a pink plastic flamingo with legs and wings of gold, glued to a small oval of plaster. The glue has long since dried out. A tiny thermometer and a piece of white coral fall off if it is moved. I put them back. Still glued to the base are two scallop shells, a fake-brass seahorse, and a little sign that says "Florida." It is a piece of junk. I should throw it out, but I like it. A real souvenir, it was brought to me by my good friend Bessie Mae Hawkins. She went on a four-day tour. On a crowded bus from Houston, it must have been a hard one, but she came home smiling with my flamingo in a pretty little box.

Bessie Mae Hawkins still looked, when I left Houston nineteen years ago, like Aunt Jemima. But she was no

Aunt Jemima. She was round with a pretty face and big, merry eyes. But she never wore an apron and wouldn't have been caught dead with a bandanna on her head. She had her hair done and wore pretty clothes. She worked for me from the time my girls were little until I left Houston, except once, when she quit me for a while. Bessie was the first household help I ever had and maybe the first paid help that anyone in my family ever had. When I was a child, Jessie, Lee Etta, and Mother Sue were given their rent and all the food my mother could manage for help with washing and ironing. Well, I forgot Lola, but she came later. She worked for my sisters in Lorenzo, Texas, and wandered around Loisie's house all day when Apollo 11 was on its way to the moon, distracted and moaning, "Moon? Moon? They gonna *think* moon!"

I thought when Bessie first came, that she had come for the day. Not so. She came to do the work and go. She had to be home when her children came from school. I learned that the hard way one day when I didn't get home until four o'clock. She came back after some months, often referring to that day as "the day you were late." I was never late again.

We were the same age, laughed at the same things, and her baby boy, Skip, was born on my birthday. How Bessie laughed at all is beyond me, her life was so hard, but she endured it with her great, grand humor. She has a delicious sense of the ridiculous.

One morning, she came in laughing, telling me a story about her neighbors down in the Third Ward. At a family gathering, they had just sat down after supper when a big rat ran into the room. They went wild, shrieking, running, and whacking until the rat was dispatched or chased out. They had fallen back into their chairs, exhausted, when a pretty little girl came up to one of her aunts, and asked, with big, widened eyes, "Did you see that gret big ol' butterfly?!"

Now Bessie and I both knew it was a sad thing that a child two or three years old, who had never owned a *Little Golden Dictionary*, didn't know a rat from a butterfly. But to us, it was funny. Sometimes there's nothing left but to laugh.

This neighbor was still cooking 'coons (raccoons) in the Third Ward in those days, and he offered Bessie's baby child, Kathy, a taste. He took the cover off a nicely roasted one. Kathy looked at it and solemnly said, "No, thank you. I don't eat monkeys." Times were changing.

Bessie and her husband, Leroy, had five children when he left her. But she never left those children. She got up at dawn, taking them to sitters or daycare when she could find it, until they were in school. When Leroy was shot (by a young woman), Bessie got a little Social Security check, the only help she ever had, that I knew of, with her children.

She was on the bus going home before they got out of school. After her early morning job, she came to my house about eleven, doing a day's work in three hours, including the ironing with my husband's starched shirts. She ironed his boxer shorts and cotton T-shirts that he wore under those starched shirts. Why did I let her do it? She once said, "Mr. Kirkpatrick is the only other man I've ever known who wanted his underwear ironed. His wife divorced *him*." I thought about it, but instead, I took the shirts to the cleaner.

We were in our forties when she began to feel ill and tired. She went to the doctor. He said she might have a tumor and ordered tests. The next week I saw her walking slowly up our driveway with the saddest look on her face. I felt a terrible chill. "She has cancer," I thought. Bessie came in and sat down. "I'm pregnant," she said. I sat down. We sat in silence for a while, or in shock, but then Bessie cheered up, as she always did, and said, "Well, I shouldn't have been surprised, as change-of-life babies runs in our family." Oh.

Near term with the baby, Bessie had to give up her jobs, but she stayed every day with my husband's mother, who was dying of cancer. "It's easy," she said. It wasn't manual labor, but it was not easy.

Bessie, pretty and sweet, had suitors. She went out with James, who was a nice man. He loved her, looked after her, and wanted to marry her, but she would not. She quit James because he took up with some "church women" who would just as soon "knife you as not." And then she met Elmo. I asked her why she wouldn't marry Elmo, also a nice man who wanted to marry her. She said, "Miz Nail, when you get married, you lose control of the situation." Bessie is a wise woman.

Kathy, her change-of-life baby, has been her most successful child, going to college, getting a good job and an apartment. Kathy married with a big church wedding. I wish I could have been there.

Bessie was a good mother and she had a good mother, Nancy Burrell. I went to Nancy's funeral, the prettiest one I've ever seen, down in the St. John Missionary Baptist Church on Gray, with beautiful women dressed in white reading eulogies, and wonderful old music sung to a huge crowd. Nancy came to Houston a young woman and settled in the Third Ward where she founded the Louisiana Social and Charity Society to help Louisiana immigrants survive in the big city. It still exists, though maybe not for that purpose.

Nancy Burrell was a wonderful cook and cooked for the Mitchell family until she died in 1973. One night she called Bessie from her work and said she was coming to Bessie's about eight thirty. She didn't show up, so Bessie called the Mitchells who said that Nancy had left on the bus at the usual time. Bessie was worried and by ten o'clock had called family, friends, and the Mitchells. They all came and fanned out through the neighborhood, up and down streets and alleys, fearing the worst. They called the police. By eleven, the police were searching and by then they were all crying, worried out of their minds. They loved that woman.

About midnight, the door opened and the despondent crowd looked up. There stood Nancy, like Lazarus, had he risen from the dead with a platter of fried fish. Nancy had met a friend coming up the street with a big catch of fish and had gone with him to help with a late-night fish fry, never dreaming anyone would worry about her. Bessie's friends, family, and the Mitchells ate the fish, laughing and crying. Fear was new in the Third Ward in those days; you had just begun to fear the worst if someone didn't come in. Today, that fear has spread all over town.

After her children were older, Bessie went from my house to the Shamrock Hotel, her third job for the day, where she cooked supper for two little boys. She did the same later for them in River Oaks, but she had to quit. Bessie required an escort to the bus stop. The gardener or somebody had to go with her to the stop and wait until the bus came. This didn't always happen and so she quit. She wasn't afraid to get off the bus in the Third Ward after dark, but she was afraid to catch it in River Oaks. She never would say why and I still don't want to know.

Bessie wasn't a fearful woman; she knew how to look after herself. It probably wasn't a physical fear that she felt in River Oaks, but something worse, racial insults or maybe ghosts. I don't know. It was spooky at night in River Oaks, down by that old Cullen mansion where the boys lived. At that time, she bought a tiny little gun that she carried in her purse. I hated it, but it stood her in good stead one morning when she was waiting for a bus with a neighbor in the Third Ward before daylight. A man in a big car stopped, got out of his car, and came toward them smiling, his hand reaching for their purses. "How are you ladies this morning?" he asked. "Just fine," replied Bessie, who was holding her little gun in front of her purse. When he saw the gun, he ran back to his car and roared away. And another time, when she didn't need the gun, she was sitting behind the bus driver when a man got on the bus and stood talking about this and that to the driver. Bessie suddenly noticed that his hand was in her purse. Her money was in her bosom, but she jumped up and began to cuss that man for everything you can imagine, insulting his mother, his looks, his mentality, until he was cowering by the door, wanting out. The driver let him out with Bessie hollering after him, "Be glad I don't have a knife or I would take your hand home in my purse!" I can see her now, putting it in a dumpster. Except for some dark thing in River Oaks, nothing intimidated Bessie.

I lived on the poor side of River Oaks near Westheimer when I left Houston, the last few years that Bessie worked for me. During that time, she was at Neiman-Marcus at six in the morning where she cleaned until ten. She loved my day, only a short bus ride from Neiman's and I think she had a good time there, making a decent wage. How she got to her second job on other days, I don't like to imagine. Her jobs were all hard. Besides my husband's underwear, she ironed dresses every week for Dot Owen's four daughters. How many miles do you suppose she pushed that iron over the years, not to speak of the mops and vacuums? By then, she had a bad heart and bad knees from all that labor for a bad wage. But she was still a happy woman, never bitter or complaining. No matter what bad time overtook her, she smiled her way through it.

Bessie came to the Third Ward when she was two years old. It was a happy, safe place. She and her brothers and sisters could play on the streets, even after dark. No doors were locked; there were no thieves or murderers. It was the same when her children grew up there, but it changed drastically with her grandchildren. Despite Bessie's great struggle to feed her children and save them from poverty, they had problems. They were poor and the schools let them down. Even at its best, the Third Ward was far from heaven.

Her first child, Nancy, so beautiful, had a problem with alcohol, nearly driving Bessie crazy, though she is in good shape now. Nancy had three children then. Bessie's mamma raised them until she died, when Bessie took over. Bessie's first boy, James, was always in trouble when he was young, but he does well today. He had three children and Bessie looked after them. I always thought Brenda was her smartest child. Very bright, she made good grades and I could see her in college, but she had a bad case of depression and didn't make it. She had four boys, whom Bessie mostly raised. One of them, Kevin, was valedictorian of his senior class. Brenda still has depression and can't live alone or work. She lives with Bessie today.

Beverly, fourth child, was a sweet girl, but when a teenager ran Bessie ragged. One night, Beverly had been out on the street or somewhere she wasn't supposed to be, far past her curfew. Bessie found her and brought her home, but was too angry to punish her until morning, when she whipped her with a belt. She came to work sick and exhausted. Love is sometimes so hard. Beverly had one child, a lovely girl, Rechale. Bessie loved and kept her. Late one night, Beverly stepped in front of a car on Cullen Boulevard. She was killed. It nearly killed Bessie. Beverly was thirty-five.

Skip, I think, was Bessie's favorite. He was darling. A funny kid, he was a perfectionist. He wanted everything to be perfect. She came in laughing after getting him off to school. He had to be dressed right. His homework had to be perfect. If the teacher wanted him to bring something for a project, it had to be just right. If it was a shoe box and Bessie had a little box, but not a shoe box, Skip wouldn't go until a shoe box was found. Bessie left the back door unlocked in case he beat her home, but nevertheless, he always gave her further instructions. "Now, if it's cold, leave the oven on and if it's raining, unlock the front door so I won't get so wet. And don't be late." Skip loved school early on, but he lost it somehow along the way and dropped out in high school. One day, he was on the front porch fussing with a young cousin. Guns had come to the Third Ward. The cousin went home and got one. He shot Skip in the eye. It was unbearable, unspeakable, and I couldn't even ask Bessie, at the time, if she was home when it happened. I heard the sound of the shot once in a dream and wondered if Bessie heard it. Of course she did. Nancy was on the porch with the boys. She ran in and told Bessie not to come out, that Skip was dead and that she must not see him. She didn't. Skip was twenty-four.

Bessie left the Third Ward and now lives out on South Braeswood. Kathy has a good job with a bank and the bank is sending her to school to finish her degree.

Kathy's husband, "cute as a button" Bessie says, has a good job with a chemical company and is also going to college. When Bessie told me that they lived with her to save money for a house, I said, "What? Who's cooking?" "Guess who!" she said, laughing one of her big laughs.

Bessie is seventy-two now, but she still works. She has a weekend job, caring for an incapacitated woman who has to be fed with a tube. "But it is easy, easy!" she said. Easy?

Bessie's life has not been easy. She has lived a Houston life, a hard life, but a happy life. Except for the days when doom ran her down like a rat out of hell. Even on those days, knowing Bessie, I imagine she got up smiling, saying to herself, "Did you see that gret big ol' butterfly?"

SEWING

I don't sew anymore. I do hem or mend something once in a great while on my Singer. Fifty years old, it has not one plastic part in its old body. It still sews a perfect seam. But I do not. The last thing I ever made on it was a tiered, circular skirt for my grand-daughter, Carrie. She was three years old and for her birthday had asked for a "pupple skut that would swul." The purple skirt was ankle length with an elastic waist, and she swirled around in it until she was seven years old.

My mother was a good seamstress, but she had no patience for it. Her feet would pound the wrought-iron pedal on her ancient Singer faster than it could go until it would jam up. She would then spend a while pulling out threads, muttering and swearing. I was her baby and when I started to school, she had no money for fabrics and patterns, but was always altering hand-me-downs. She would sew up my dress on the sides, taking many inches off each, leaving the shoulders large and strange. Skinny as a rail, I looked as if I had giant shoulder pads, in the days when women wore none.

My Aunt Gus, a more careful, cautious woman than her sister Kate, took pity on me. When I was in elementary school she made me three dresses every fall. From one pattern, they had long, puffed sleeves, a fitted waist, and the skirts swirled. I never minded their being alike, the print the same except for the colors, red, blue, and green. I loved them and chose, each day, the one to wear by the color, according to my mood.

I carefully hung them up afternoons, putting on my old coveralls for play. I wanted to delay their washings and to preserve their beautiful newness as long as possible. Aunt Gus had four kids of her own and she finally had to give up making me dresses. Except for one, I had no new ones for a long time after Gus.

When I was about twelve, Ma somehow made for me at Christmas a white velveteen dress, with little pom-poms of rabbit fur sewn on the ends of the sash. Beautifully made, a perfect fit, I don't know how she did it. Lord, what I wouldn't give for a picture of it, but we had no camera. Had we had one, for all these pictures in my mind's eye I would need a warehouse.

Once I was in an airport in line for boarding with Carrie, who was nearly three and in a new dress. She held the bottom of her skirt up to a woman sitting nearby and asked, "Would you like to smell my new dress?" A man behind me was amused and he laughed. I turned to him and said, "She loves the smell of new clothes and so do I."

The department stores in Houston when I was young and sewing all had large fabric departments, with long, high counters full of pattern books. We sat on stools for hours poring over those books with children clambering around at our feet, some stretched out moaning on the floor, all wanting to go home.

I wish I had taken mine home and forgotten the whole thing, but I was young and foolish and didn't know that fashion could kill. It is a dangerous business for models today as some die of starvation to meet the requirements of fashion. I have an old picture of my daughter Leslie and it nearly kills me to look at it. She was crying because she had to go to a party or because she had to wear a stiff, organdy dress I had made for Easter. I wish I knew which. I wish I hadn't made her wear it. The dress had a ruffled collar, a tight bodice, little puffed sleeves, and a big petticoat. It was hot. We dressed our children up for parties then. Now she would be in shorts and T-shirt. Mothers are wiser about such things today. Our lives were measured out, not with coffee spoons like Prufrock's, but with Easter dresses, hats, gloves, petticoats, and patent leather shoes.

My friend Dot Owen is the only master seamstress I have known. She has four daughters, grown now, praise God. Dot was and is an artist at sewing and choosing fabrics, colors, and patterns for it. If all of the perfect clothes that she has made were paid for at their true value and laid end to end. . . . Never mind. She would be an exceedingly rich woman.

It is a miracle that she walks around so erect today in her seventies. Just to think of the shorts, shirts, pants, nightgowns, dresses, costumes and God only knows what else that she made for four daughters and their children nearly puts me in bed. Once for a May Fête at Cunningham Elementary in Bellaire, she made costumes for Jeni and Betsy and for two children who had no mother. The motherless children didn't show for the May Fête. And in recent times, she made costumes for granddaughter Sarah, who was in the Houston Children's Chorus. Except for a tutu I made for Leslie to wear in a ballet recital, the only costumes I can recall were two black cat suits I made for Halloween. The bodies were easy, but the ears and the long tails took me two afternoons. After that, Les and Kate went trick-or-treating as ghosts until they were old enough to devise their own costumes. They were darling cats, though.

Not so long ago, Dot made a junior-bridesmaid dress for her granddaughter Anna to wear in her uncle's big wedding. Anna, eight, only measured 22-22-22 and Dot had to adapt a child's size six pattern to fit skinny Anna and redesign it, lengthening the waist and all until it looked right for a very small bridesmaid. To accomplish this she made two practice dresses. Anna came just before the wedding. The dress fit her to perfection, but, alas, was too long. The bottom of the waist and skirt were finished with embroidered, scalloped eyelet. It had to be lifted from the waist. Nothing to do but take it apart, zipper, lining, and all. And then, after the wedding, this was done again to shorten it to Sunday school length. Just to think of it makes me want to lie down somewhere with a cold, wet rag on my forehead.

I hope Anna is saving that beautiful, priceless dress for her children and their children. I don't think Dot will ever make another. Dot, to this day, has a funny thing about boxes from a trauma she suffered as second-grade room mother. The teacher had approached her, smiling, with a large box. In the box was heavy-duty canvas for twenty-four bookbags. The teacher said she knew Dot wouldn't mind finding some mothers to help her make them. Dot thought about the week it would take to drag enough mothers from under their beds and made them herself, breaking twelve needles in the process and ruining her disposition for weeks. Even now, if someone comes smiling with a box, she clenches her fists behind her back, grits her teeth, and walks backward. Her daughters grew up to be editor, doctor, lawyer, and school principal. I doubt they own sewing machines.

My friend Dorothy Robertson, like most of us, only sewed because she had to. She called me one morning to come help her. She had done something peculiar to a dress she was making for daughter Karen. The instructions said to sew the dress and sleeve seams "all in one," meaning, after the sleeve was set into the shoulder, to start at the bottom of the dress and sew up the side seam and out to the end of the sleeve seam. Dorothy had carefully inserted the sleeve seam into the side seam and sewn them "all in one," making a neat little straitjacket. Karen was walking around in it with a wild look in her eyes. I thought Dorothy should keep it, as Karen, about three, was a child with a mind of her own, a polite way of saying stubborn as a mule. She was large for her age and a terror in downtown Foley's. The only Foley's in town, it could be unbelievably crowded. Dorothy and I would drag our girls around that store unmercifully until Karen had enough. She would lie down on the floor under all the feet, stretching across the aisle as limp as a rag, except for her feet, which were kicking everything in reach. It took us both to get her up. The dress would have helped, or better, pants with the inseams sewn all in one.

Karen, who was a head taller than anyone in her class until she was ten, grew up to be a small, sweet woman, but she still has a mind of her own. She is a fraud expert and works with the FBI, giving seminars about document fraud. And she sews! Her sister, Susie, is a lawyer. She sings, but she does not sew.

Like Ma, I had no patience for sewing. I was challenged by the learning how, but it was grim work after that, except for the pleasure in the product. I traumatized Leslie when she was little. I had nearly finished pinning the pattern on some expensive, pale silk spread out on my bedroom floor. Les was watching with a big glass of red Kool-Aid. She dropped the glass. Plastic, it bounced all over that silk, the red spreading and soaking through the tissue of the pattern with its sticky, strawberry sweetness. I fell over backward and threw a raving fit. I went absolutely mad. Les, an intelligent child, took off for the backyard and hid behind the oleanders. I wasn't yelling at her, just yelling, but if she could retrieve that day from her repressed memory, she could have me arrested for child abuse. I finally finished the dress, but I hated it.

When my daughters were very small I made their dresses alike. When Katy was to go to kindergarten I made dresses of the same fabric, but Katy's was a little smock with an apron. I cut out a little duck and appliquéd it for a pocket on the apron. Katy didn't like it; she said it was a baby dress. I took her to school on the first day, and she said, "Now, Mamma, don't come to meet me. I know the way home." Kolter Elementary was only around the block, but I began to worry that she would be disoriented and would go in the wrong direction. So I waited at the corner when school was out. She saw me, ran past and began to cry. She cried all the way home and she walked around the house, crying and beating her breast all afternoon, like the heroine at the end of a tragic opera. "You have turned me back into a baby," she sobbed over and over, "with this baby apron and baby duck and coming to get me." So much trauma and drama for an afternoon spent appliquéing, by hand, a white duck on a blue apron. Katy and Les, painter and poet, do not sew.

The last thing my mother made for me was a skirt for my trousseau. She had given it her all and it was pretty. Brown and white checked cotton, it was long and full with a ruffle. I was wearing it in Houston in 1948 the first time I caught a bus and went downtown in that big city. I was going to meet my husband and Helen Corbett for lunch. Paul was supervising the air-conditioning and mechanical engineering for a building that Joskes' furniture store was remodeling. Helen Corbett, a chef soon to be famous for her good food and best-selling cookbooks, had come to manage the lunch room. Paul helped her with her kitchen and they became great friends. We went dancing with Helen out on South Main.

Walking down Main Street on that lovely June day, I was excited by the crowds and the big buildings. I felt so fortunate to have a handsome husband to meet for lunch and, if I do say so, I was one good-looking woman. My face wasn't all that much, but I was blessed with a marvelous, perfect body. My legs were gorgeous. In fact, I was stunning in my skirt, white peasant blouse, and my new brown and white, high-heeled spectator pumps. As happy as a lark, I was passing the Rice Hotel when I noticed that people were giving me a wide berth and looking at me oddly. I glanced down and saw my knees hanging out. Trailing far behind me, like a long tail, was my ruffle, which Ma had only basted on. I went in Woolworth's, bought straight pins, and pinned the ruffle back on, then proceeded on my way, looking not quite so grand.

Paul took one look and said, "What happened to your skirt?" Helen Corbett burst out laughing. At lunch, I was careful not to sit on the pins.

Where was my Aunt Gus when I needed her? Deliver me, Lord, not from evil, but from sewing.

SPACE

Nothing troubles me more than time and space;
yet nothing troubles me less,
as I never think about them.

Charles Lamb

I have learned to live with time, but space troubles me no end. I read Genesis when I was eight years old. I believed that God made light on the first day and on the fourth he hung the moon, sun, and stars in their places. And then I learned that they weren't hung on little hooks, but were loose out there and so were we. As a child, I knew the earth was round and moving, that I could dig a hole right down to China. I dug many a hole, never got there, but knew I could. I thought that one day, gravity would let go and we would all fly off into the sky. I didn't look forward to

135

it. My gang down on South Seventh Street hoped that we would be flung off to the moon, where the moon people would ask, "Where ya'll from?"

Today, I try not to think about space, the universe, and the black holes. "O, that way madness lies," Lear said of something else, but it's true of space. I read of the constant new discoveries out there in what we call "our" space. My painting teacher, Dorothy Hood, called it the "void." She pondered it incessantly and painted world famous paintings about it. When I do think of it, I see Dürer's engraving, *Melencolia I,* of the big old brooding angel with her great puzzled eyes staring into space. It was done after his mother's death in 1514. Many have tried to figure it out since then. And so have I. There she sits, distraught and disheveled, yet her keys on a chain and her purse at her feet are symbols of power and wealth, according to Dürer. On her lap is a closed book. I think it's the Bible. In her hand, a compass, a symbol of knowledge. Behind her, a cherub sits on a millstone, writing in a book, maybe keeping tabs on her doubt and faith. On the wall above his head, a scale, sometimes a symbol of the true and false, and an hourglass, of course, to measure time or the lack of it, and a bell to toll it. An old hound, her only comfort, sleeps at her feet and nearby is a sphere and a granite polyhedron. She knows too much. And under a rainbow, what may have finished her off, a brilliant comet from out of nowhere and on its way to nowhere. This engraving has had thousands of interpretations, but most agree she is the artistic genius, despairing of inspiration. Hogwash. She is simply an angel whose knowledge is shaking her faith, making her very, very melancholy.

Who, indeed, could be more melancholy than a faithless angel? Her melancholy (or Dürer's) speaks to a mysterious sadness, to what Joseph Conrad called the loneliness of us all, from the cradle to the grave. Dürer said of his angel that she was a woman "from whose eyes Saturn looks out." That gives me a bad case of goose bumps. The Saturn Dürer referred to was not the god of agriculture, but the planet Saturn, which represents the negative aspects of destiny, not only in Western astrology, but also that of the Hindus. In fact, when the Hindu mountain goddess, Parvati, had her baby, Ganapati, (I just love their names) Saturn didn't offer to look at him for fear of hurting him. His mother asked Saturn to gaze on him so he would know adversity. Adversity? His gaze burned that kid's head plumb off. It was replaced with an elephant's head and that is why, in Hindu mythology, we have this funny looking little old god. But the eyes of Dürer's angel, from which Saturn looks, are magical, even in a book. They have a terrible gaze. No telling how they might be in the original engraving, which I think is in the Fogg Museum at Harvard. If I ever get there to see it, I won't look long into those Saturn eyes, for fear my head might begin to glow.

And then there is the comet Hale-Bopp, which came along to plague me in my old age at the end of the twentieth century. It was fun, at first, to see it. One night, I had my best view at the Lady Bird Johnson Wildflower Center, south of Austin. The prettiest spring that I can remember, the wildflowers there that night lit up the earth, and above the glowing flowers, in the darkest sky you could find, was the comet, on its way to the end of forever. For an instant, in that heavenly place, I wanted to shout, "Take me, take me!"

I remember a story in the *Texas Monthly*; I don't know who wrote it. The writer was in a giant Baptist church, maybe in Fort Worth, when a choir of hundreds marched down every aisle, singing in one thunderous voice, "Oh who will come and go with me, I am bound for the promised land?" As I remember, it was all he could do not to run after them, shouting, "Take me, take me."

I read that one of Hale-Bopp's tails is about 373,000 miles wide and 31 million miles long and it's farther from us than we are from the sun. And one of its tails could fill the Great Lakes with ice. I don't want to know about it. Don't tell me any more. I'm about Hale-Bopp as my granddaughter, Carrie, was about crocodiles. When she was two, we took her to the zoo in San Antonio, where all grandchildren must go. We were walking down a path when I saw the crocodile, smiling, teeth bare, right at our feet, a little wall around him. "Look! There's a crocodile," I said as I picked her up and held her just above him. "Oh, please," she said, closing her eyes, "Don't let me see that crocodile!" As we hurried away, she called to him over my shoulder, "Don't eat *me*. Don't eat *me*."

Oh, please. Don't let me see that comet. And don't take me. Don't take me.

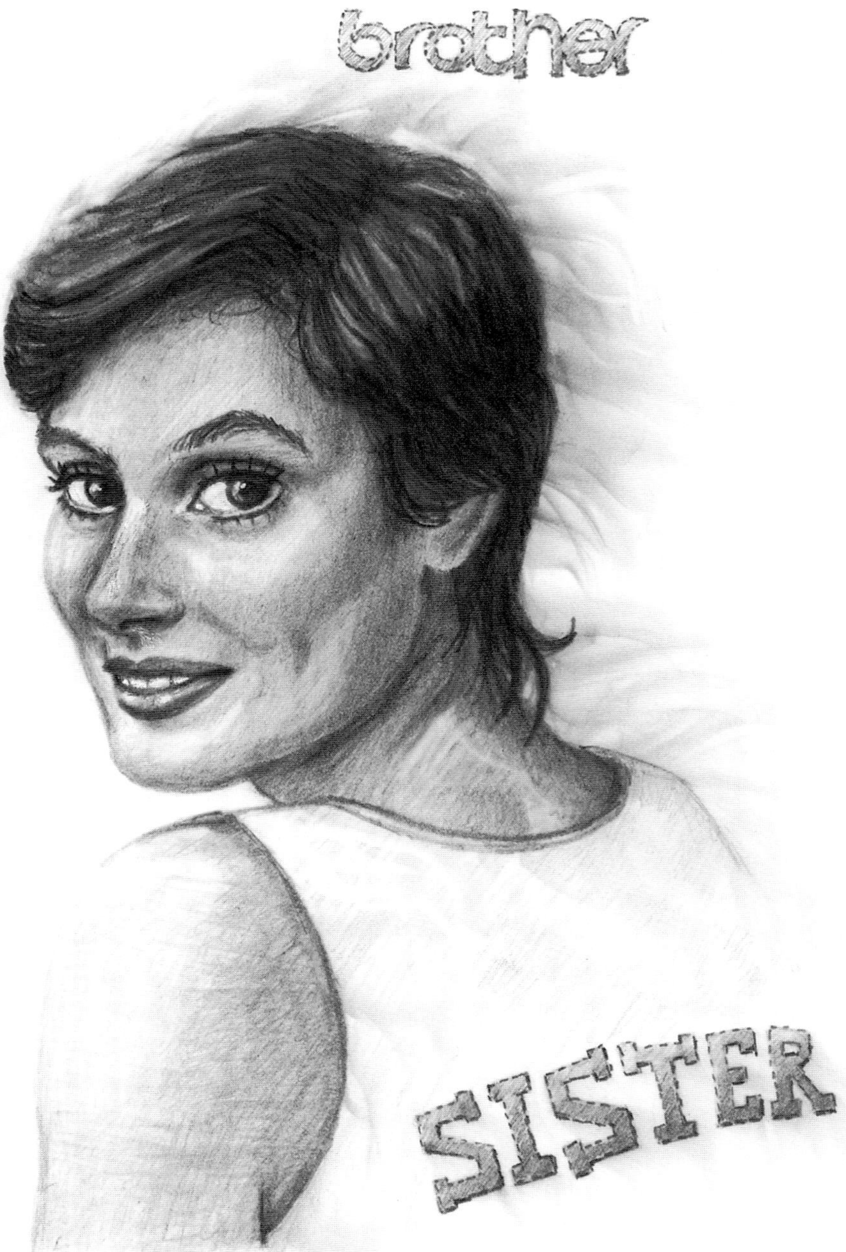
brother
SISTER

TIME

I have drunk ale from the Country of the Young
And weep because I know all things now.

W.B. Yeats

I doubt that Dylan Thomas was on Yeats' wavelength when he wrote about the sun that is young once only and of time that lets us play and be "golden in the mercy of his means." Such as they are. I once painted a dark painting about that line. Called it *Golden in the Mercy*. It won something from the Texas Fine Arts Association. I forget what. A collector wanted it, but not enough to pay its worth. I still have it. The time was out of joint when I went to art school at forty and I was not born to put it right. The desirable "emerging artists," when I was in my forties, were twenty, according to the critics and galleries. And so, limping along and beginning to write in my seventies with the time still out of joint, I know now I will never put it right.

Sometimes, when I feel like a stranger on this earth, a line from an old poem devils me: "The world is not my home, boys, I'm only passing through." I began to lose the world years ago when I gave up commercial television and returned to radio and reading. Oh, I watch a few special things off and on, barely able to endure the commercials with their coughs, snorts, and drips from noses and other places. Actually, I never gave up books or radio, but at night I watched television with the rest of the world. Now, I listen all day to public radio. I do watch Jim Lehrer's news hour on PBS and whatever they send my way before I go to bed to read. But I no longer understand the conversation when I sit with friends discussing their favorite programs and commercials. And their computers. I am lost, listening to a foreign language. Oh, I know all about snakes, squid, sharks, whales, and the sexual habits of every known monkey in the world, but I have learned not to bring them up. It casts a pall over the room.

I am a stranger, though, in a strange land. I kept a *New Yorker* cartoon from the sixties until it was a faded shambles the last time I saw it. A stately woman was carrying a sign in a crowd of young protesters. Hers said, "Will someone please tell me what is going on?" I knew what was "going on" in the sixties. I was not yet forty when they came. I fell right in with them, though I did have a problem with the way the kids looked. The boys, with their unkempt hair and long old men's beards, looked like weak old men. The girls had to have straight hair. If it was curly, they ironed it on ironing boards, slaves to fashion as women have always been and ever will be. Hair parted in the middle, faces unadorned and obscured by hair and wire-framed glasses, they looked like those poor women who walked behind the wagons to California during the first great migration, worn to a nub.

It seemed to me if you had a great cause the least you could do for it was to look your best. Thank God, I no longer worry about such things. I haven't understood much since the early eighties, especially the language. If I were to march today, looking as good as an old woman can look, my placard would read, "What did you say?" or maybe just, "What?"

I haven't understood any technical thing since I was six years old. Not even radio and telephone. Voices coming through the air and over wires? Oh, come on! I don't even understand this simple little word processor that I am using right this minute. When I began to write at seventy, my daughter Les made me buy it because my ancient typewriter wouldn't double-space. She spent three days pounding on me until I could use it. When I first turned it on, I was asked to type my name and a message appeared on the screen. It said, "Hello, Frances, I am your Brother and I am here to help you." Well, he is my brother and he has helped me. I know he's in there. Don't tell me any more.

Television is beyond comprehension. Imagine what will happen to us with the digital TV, which is supposed to be standard in 2006. They say the picture will be so sharp that you will see every detail and flaw. I shudder at the thought of the drips and snorts. God only knows what will happen to *Casablanca* and the *African Queen*. Unless our black hole gets us, I will only be eighty-two. But I won't see it. I will be glued to my radio, my only constant, which has endured and will endure forever. Oh, please. Don't let me see digital television.

Being a time addict, never without a watch and always on time, I do understand time. My watch is not digital, but has a face and hands. I want to see the time past and the time to come. And the clocks I have known. Old alarm clocks, big and round with bells on top ticking away in quiet old houses in quiet old towns. A loud incessant ticking away of time, one clock heard all over the house in the dead of night. And the old Seth Thomas clocks of carved oak, their pendulums tick-tock tick-tocking away and their tolling of the hour and half hour. In her old age, my mother had her auntie's clock. I heard that clock as a child in her old dogtrot house in the country out of Kosse. It didn't have a lovely chime, but like all of those old oak clocks, it boomed and clanged, as if someone were hitting a gong. Fifty years later, I heard it in my mother's house out in Lorenzo, near Lubbock, telling me that it was four o'clock in the morning and that my mother's time was short.

My husband inherited a Seth Thomas clock from his grandmother (he called her Miss Liny) and her clock sat on our mantel with the same old rattle and bang at the hour. My children grew up with it, but time means nothing to children. There is so much of it then. Christmas never comes, school is never out, and summer never ends. At least that was the way it was in the old days. Time began to change for my kids, but except for dinnertime, suppertime, and bedtime, it meant nothing to me when I was a child. Well, I do recall one hot summer day right after noon, when I, about five, rapped loudly on the back door of my new friend, who had just moved back from California to South Seventh Street. Mrs. Tarver came to the door, her finger on her lips. "Can Winifred Jane and Don Q. come out?" I loudly asked. "Shush!" she whispered. "Don't you take naps?" "No, Ma'am," I said, but I was so embarrassed I ran home and found my mother. She was on the bed reading the *Ladies' Home*

Journal. I snuggled up by her side and went to sleep. On that day, I began to watch the clock.

When we were barely teenagers, we were allowed to go to the midnight movie on Saturday nights, to come home immediately after, usually walking. One night, Jane Harris, a beautiful girl from out in the country, came in to go with us, four or five girls to be driven home by a wild boy from Lakeview. He was to take Jane home last, because she lived so far away. But he said to us, "Let's all drive out to Jane's, and I will bring you back." "Let's go!" we said, showing no sign yet of intelligence. So, about four, we arrived at our first stop back in Memphis at Peggy George Walker's house. Her father, Red, a man whose word was law, red-headed, a wide man, was sitting on the front steps, like a great Buddha, still as glass. He didn't move when we stopped, but Saturn looked out of his eyes. Except for Peggy George, we all sank down into the seats to escape his gaze. And just at that moment, Chick Gerlach's mother roared around the corner in her old gray Plymouth, honking and shouting, having been searching for us for two hours. Time caught up with us that night.

The most mortifying time I had with time happened one night after I went on a picnic out at a lake. Barely thirteen and easily embarrassed, I was supposed to be home at ten. I don't remember that picnic, but I remember arriving in front of our rented, brown house down on Seventh Street around eleven, not with the mother that took me, but in the back of a pickup loaded with kids. I knew my mother was sleeping in the front bedroom, her head at the window. "Ma," I shouted, "we're back and we're going to ride around awhile." My mother's voice, when she was really aggravated, could be heard for miles. "GET OUT OF THAT TRUCK, YOU LITTLE FOOL!" I jumped out like a "bat out of glory," her expression for speed. It was one of my worst encounters with time.

I still love time, though, and all of its seasons, but I have begun to talk to my clock. I worry about it. Well, it is a talking clock. Many have them, but do they talk to their clocks? I don't think so. It is supposed to be a digital recording, whatever that is. But I don't believe it. How do I know a little Japanese time sprite or elf didn't take up residence in my clock? She has the sweetest little voice. I know she's in there. When I punch her button, she hates to tell me, but says with a sigh, "It's three-thirty A.M." I say, "Gosh, I hoped it was morning, but thanks anyway, dear." Or she says, "It's eight o'clock A.M." and I reply, "Oh Lord, I should have been up at six. But thank you, sweet thing, for the time." I do love my talking clock, be-cause Miss Liny's old oak clock quit bonging out to me the night hours and half hours years ago. It sits silent on a kitchen counter, no longer tick-tocking away my time.

My generation was the last, like the children in "Fern Hill," allowed by time, in the "sun born over and over," to run our heedless ways. And I remember some of my old bunch, who rode in the back of a pickup late one night down South Seventh Street in Memphis, Texas, out in the Red River Valley on the Prairie Dog Fork of the Red at the foot of the Palo Duro Canyon on the third planet from the sun. It was a long time ago and my memory is flaky, and the only ones I can see, of the crowd in the bed of the truck, are George Carter, Bobby Lindsey, Charlene Gerlach, Neysa Nell Coursey, Polly Sanders, Patsy Ruth Hall, Rosalyn Watson, and me. Rosalyn probably wasn't there, already moved to Lubbock, no doubt, but I never see my old bunch without seeing Rosalyn in my mind's eye. So blond, so fair, so good, so beautiful, our Snow White. She didn't last long in this world, for no handsome prince came to wake her.

Time, after all, showed us no mercy. Only Polly and I are still here. Time, cancer, and alcohol took the rest too young. We were a fragile bunch of earthlings.

No wonder, then, that when my little sprite tells me sadly that it's four o'clock in the morning, I feel Saturn looking out of my eyes into the darkness and, like an unwelcome parade from an old Fellini movie, comes a slow procession of old sorrows, old sins, old loves, old women leaning over pots and pans full of turnip greens and black-eyed peas, old regrets, old trees, old picnics, old porches, old yards, old creeks, old cars, old roads. Old dogs. No wonder, then, to hasten the exit of this motley parade, I consider, for a while, old poems and repeat their old lines over and over, like a mantra.

Dylan Thomas's "Fern Hill" may be the most beautiful poem ever written of childhood and of time and his sad lines bear repeating. "Nothing I cared," he said, "in the lamb white days, that time would take me." It is comforting in the black night to slip back into the "lamb white days," but at that hour and at my age, I call up W.B. Yeats, the King of the Midnight Saviors. His old poems will wash away your sins and replace them with far better ones of his own. He caught a little silver trout that turned into a "glimmering girl" with an apple blossom in her hair. She called him by his name "and ran and faded through the brightening air." He wandered until he was old, searching and always expecting to "kiss her lips and take her hands; and walk among long dappled grass, and pluck till time and times are done the silver apples of the moon, the golden apples of the sun." And Yeats will take you sailing to the holy city of Byzantium. His country was no country for the old, with the young in one another's arms and the birds in the trees. Where "fish, flesh, or fowl commend all summer long, whatever is begotten, born, and dies." And where "caught in that sensual music, all neglect monuments of unaging intellect." And so he sailed to Byzantium.

There was a bird in Byzantium, made by Grecian goldsmiths, of hammered gold and gold enamelling. It was set upon a golden bough to sing to the lords and ladies of Byzantium of what is past, or passing, or to come.

PRAYER

The last night I ever slept in the same house with my daddy, I heard his old whisper, "Our Father who art in heaven. . . ." He was nearly ninety and I had heard him whisper that prayer since my memory began. He would get into bed, lie on his back, clasp his hands over his chest, and after a time of silence would pray in a very loud whisper. I could never make out the words, but I knew from the cadence that it was the Lord's Prayer.

When we children were small, we slept scattered around. We never had rooms of our own. When we were all in bed, my mother's voice would call out across the house, "Now I lay me down to sleep." We would answer line for line, "I pray the Lord my soul to keep. If I should die before I wake, I pray the Lord my soul to take." We were strong on the third line; we already knew about dying.

I don't pray as much as I did when I was young, but sometimes I find myself flat on my back in bed, my hands clasped over my chest in silence. Then I mutter and mumble to myself awhile, praying that God will hear me.

I don't remember ever praying in class at school. I don't remember our teachers praying, though I'm sure some of them prayed silently, asking God to save them from violence. Not our violence, but theirs, for I'm sure some of them wanted to kill us. We did have prayers sometimes for assembly in the school auditorium. For important occasions a preacher would be there for the opening prayer. But we didn't listen. We were so happy to be out of class that we spent the prayer time jabbing ribs and making faces, trying to force someone to laugh out loud and holding our noses so it wouldn't be us.

One of our favorite family prayers was handed down from my Aunt Grace. We still say it as a last resort, when there are no words for the situation: "Lord." (Long pause.) "Lord?" (Long pause.) "Now, oh Lord."

She didn't say "Lord." She said "Law-erd." That's all there is to the prayer, but it comes in handy. Aunt Grace was at a revival up in Kosse when she was just a girl, shy and very pretty. The preacher called on her. "Sister Grace, will you lead us in prayer?" Grace repeated her prayer over and over and over—*Lord, Lord, now, oh Lord*—until someone mercifully took pity on her and prayed. But not before her brothers were rolling in the grass, holding their sides and kicking and laughing. They never let her live it down, often saying, "Sister Grace will lead us in prayer." When I knew Aunt Grace, she was never at a loss for words. I know she prayed, but I'm pretty certain she never again prayed aloud in public.

I've never held with fundamentalist prayers asking for new tires, health, wealth, and happiness. I've always felt that if God gave those things to one of us, he would give them to all of us. But my sister Bob became a fundamentalist in her middle age, aggravating my Methodist mother no end. Bob's old car wore out and she had to have another, which she couldn't afford. She had a country newspaper and needed the car for her business. I was worried about it, but Bob said, "Not to worry, the Lord will provide."

I lived in Houston then and always called Ma in Lubbock on Monday mornings. One Monday I asked Ma if Bob had gotten a car. "Yes," Ma said, "she just drove in. God has given the fool a Lincoln Continental!" It was one of those car stories, only true. An old woman had sold Bob this elegant car with twenty thousand miles for practically nothing. The old woman wore heavy perfume and Bob complained, with a lack of grace, that the car ever after smelled of Shalomar. Bob drove that car for years until it was a heap, still smelling of Shalomar. Before Janis Joplin, she used to joke that someday God would give her a Mercedes Benz. When Ma was gone, I was calling Bob on Monday mornings. One morning I asked what she was going to do that day. She said, "Drive out in my Mercedes Benz!" A born-again friend of hers had actually given her one. She drove it awhile and then gave it back. She said it was too much to ask of God.

Ma's little sister, my Aunt Ruth, was the only truly good person that I have ever known. No old people in our family ever lacked for care if they lived near Ruth. She was poor but she gave what she had to anyone in need. She prayed night and day for others, never for herself. She is the only person I've ever known who had her prayers answered, or at least one of them. Her dearly loved niece was running around with a man that Ruth considered bad and very unsuitable. Ruth said that she woke up one morning about three-thirty, terribly "burdened" for Nelma. She prayed until four o'clock, asking God to remove this man from Nelma's life. Ruth learned the next morning that the man had been shot at four-thirty in a honky-tonk. She prayed again. "Forgive me, Lord. I didn't mean for you to kill him."

Ma loved Ruth so, but she also loved to aggravate

her. She teased her about her total dependence on God. "Don't you imagine, Ruthie, that God is just sick of your voice? Nag, nag, nag, day and night!" Actually, Ruth was thrilled with Ma's brazen talk and ugly words. Never having said a bad word in her life, she would hold her nose and turn her head to hide her laughing.

Ruth was a good writer and wrote many, many letters, but she often had no stamps. Once, when they were as old as the hills, Ma sent her a sheet of stamps. Ruth was not a pious woman; she was full of fun. She wrote Ma and said, "Guess what? God has sent me one hundred stamps!" Ma called her. "You little shit," she said. "You know God didn't send you those stamps!"

Now Ma never used that word except for a cuss word, and the telephone call would have been shock enough. They wrote volumes of letters, but calls were for emergencies. About the worst thing Ma ever called a person was "little rat turd," and that was a term of endearment. "Get out of those cookies, you little rat turd."

When I was about thirteen, Gypsy Smith, a famous English revivalist, came to Memphis. Oh, it was exciting! Here was this great man, a real Gypsy, all the way from England over the ocean and on the trains across America, standing on the stage in the high school auditorium in Memphis, Texas. He preached to the public at eleven-thirty; the people overflowed into the halls. He preached to every white child in Memphis at one-thirty. He said he was uneducated and when he was converted, he couldn't write his name. Of this much I am certain because I wrote it in my diary. The rest, I remember.

I see him in a white suit. I don't know if he wore one, but he had Mark Twain hair, and Twain wore one. He wasn't like Twain, though. He was big and swarthy as a Gypsy should be and he had great, dark, piercing eyes. He pinned us to our seats with them. He strode onto the stage and then stood in silence, looking into our souls with those eyes. After a great while, he recited an ancient rhyme:

> *My mother said I never should*
> *Play with Gypsies in the wood.*

I began to have the most delicious thoughts about playing with Gypsies in the wood and about why my mother wouldn't like it. And then I realized that his finger was pointing straight at me and he was shouting, "Let not one dark spot stain your pure mind. Wash it out! Wash it out!" I suddenly pictured a little faucet in the top of my head. I turned it on and washed my little mind until it was as white as snow. I used that faucet for years to rid myself of unwelcome thoughts. It would take a fire hose today to wash the dark spots from my old brain.

I met a woman once, thankfully only once, who was talking about her prayer life and her relationship with God. She said she prayed every morning on her knees for thirty minutes, asking God for guidance for this day that he had given her. The day I met her, God had told her to do something about her living room. She had found this wonderful chair. This is the day that the Lord hath made. Great God of us all, what shall I do with it? "Go shopping."

I would be afraid to pray for anything today except forgiveness. Forgive us for the guns on our streets and the lost children. Forgive us because our great nation, under God, is the foremost maker and seller of weapons on this earth. Lord, now oh Lord. Mea culpa.

Old Turgenev, a Russian poet and novelist from long ago, had it right. His peers scorned him. One of them said that he wrote with one finger pointing to the tear in his eye. He said more than a hundred years ago that no matter what we pray for, we are praying for a miracle. He said that every prayer reduces itself to this: "Great God grant that twice two be not four."

GOD

For fear of God, I was a virgin until I was twenty-four years old. It was the custom in the old days to wait for sex until you were married or old enough to tell the difference between true life and a hole in the ground, whichever came first. My high school friends were also as pure as the driven snow as far as I knew, for fear of talk, if not for fear of God.

We believed the story of Adam and Eve and we believed they heard the voice of God as he walked in the garden in the cool of the evening. We were brought up in church, believing every word of the Bible, our heads full of fire, brimstone, and fright from too many revivals with wild old preachers scaring us to virtue. We believed in sin. An unwed pregnant girl was rare and even a bad reputation caused much weeping and wailing and guilt and shame.

Sex, cigarettes, and whiskey were the three vices to my old bunch. We didn't drink or smoke in high school, though many boys and some girls did. Oh, we sometimes would sneak cigarettes and hide out in the country, smoking and giggling until we were too dizzy to stand, but we knew it was a *sinful* thing to do. Sex was always on our minds and at slumber parties we talked about it endlessly in low voices, shivering at the thought of it. Fear and guilt may be bad things and I know that sex is not the sin that we once thought, but our lives were simpler and certainly healthier than those of some teens today. For whatever reason I was chaste, for fear of God or just plain fear, I've never regretted it. I felt impudent, independent, and even noble when I was still a virgin.

It was easier to fear God when he was talking all the time, telling people what to do and what not to do. A voice from heaven today would send us to a psychiatrist. When Elijah, the only man still alive who knew God, was being hounded down by Ahab and that ratty Jezebel, who really wanted to do him in, and he was hiding out, starving, God sent ravens and an angel to bring him food and drink. God doesn't do that anymore; the hounded in our world starve.

Elijah made it to a cave on a holy mountain and waited to hear from God. The Bible says that a great wind came, strong enough to tear the mountain apart, an earthquake strong enough to shake it to pieces, and a great fire. But God wasn't in the wind, earthquake, or fire. After the fire, Elijah heard a "still, small voice."

Now Jezebel worshipped Baal, the god of fertility and nature, and she had killed all of the prophets of Yahweh, as God was called then. She was Phoenician and Baal was a Phoenician god. Her husband, Ahab, built an ivory house in Samaria where people "lay on ivory beds and sprawled on their divans." Jezebel came to a bad end, thrown over an ivory balustrade, run over by a horse, and eaten by dogs. I doubt God did it; I suspect soldiers. After Elijah heard the still, small voice, the Bible says that God killed all but seven thousand in Israel, all but those who did not bow the knee to Baal and who did not kiss his feet. I don't believe a word of it. They put the blame on God, but God didn't kill those people—hate and war did it. It is the same today, same as it ever was. In war and hate, if we win, we say that God is on our side.

We blame God and give him credit where neither is due. A woman who survived the airplane crash in Dallas some years ago said, "It was the goodness of God. God's goodness and mercy saved us all." I wonder why she thought the one hundred thirty-seven who died did not deserve that goodness and mercy. The wind shear killed them, not God. Luck saved the rest. Suppose two children are near death in a burn ward, one with a family and a whole church praying constantly, one with nobody. Would God save the loved or the unloved? Who could love a God who has to be bought off with pleading and praise?

I don't go to church much anymore, but I believe in God. I believe in the Father, Son, and Holy Ghost. Why, I don't know. Faith, I suppose. Faith is like the flu, hard to shake. I think God is more omnipotent and unknowable than we ever dreamed, beyond the power of our little bitty minds. I am certain, though, that he is not my good old great grandpa and he is *not* going to save me from evil.

The still, small voice that Elijah heard has been interpreted to mean a "sound of silence." We will not hear it. Our world is too noisy with its streets full of gunfire and its leaf blowers, boomboxes, bulldozers, bombers, bombs, screaming children, and crying babies.

Even the churches are noisy. I visited a new version of my old church. The music was good and I sat in the quiet of it, beginning to feel receptive and even worshipful. The minister prayed a thoughtful prayer and I was silent and listening, when suddenly everyone jumped up, hugging and shaking hands, introducing themselves and smiling fake smiles. I tried to stay in my seat but was dragged upright by firm, but friendly, hands. No reverence allowed in this house of the Lord. The sweet children came to the altar and said cute things for our entertainment. We laughed. One of the hardest lessons I learned from my old church as a child was to be quiet and to listen. And then names were called out, as at an auction, of those needing prayer and we prayed for them. All I could think of were those in need who had no one to speak their names. Unprayed for, were they left off God's help list that day? Then someone gave a talk about something and the minister preached a short and beautiful sermon. But I had lost it by then.

And in some churches people wave their arms in the air, to attract God's attention I guess. I know it attracts mine. Jesus is sold in their market places in cassettes, books, cards, and screen-savers for computers at a great profit, unforetold by prophets. And now we have the "Jesus bracelet," with W.W.J.D. (what would Jesus do?) imprinted on it. They cost about two dollars. If someone asks why you wear it, you explain and give him your bracelet, buying another for yourself. If you wear it, you must live the way Jesus lived. They come in eight colors and there are W.W.J.D. hats and jeans with embroidered letters and coming, of course, are the T-shirts. The man who is marketing all this says it is the work of God. From what I read, about a million will have been sold by the end of this year, so figure another million, at least, next year. *I love it.* Can you imagine what two million people, wearing these bracelets, doing as Jesus would do, living as Jesus lived, will do for this country? Abused children will be cared for and loved, the homeless will be housed, the hungry will be fed, and the schizophrenics will be returned to much kinder hospitals than we threw them onto the streets from years ago.

Shout hallelujah! But don't hold your breath.

In some churches there is even shouting, dancing, and singing and people fall prone at the altar and speak in unknown tongues. And something curious is creeping down from Canada in the Pentecostal churches. Called the Toronto Blessing, it is supposed to be the last great visit of the Holy Spirit before the end of the world. This blessing requires teams of catchers, to catch those slain in the spirit before they hit the floor, to prevent broken bones. One story I read about it said a young man was jogging endlessly, back and forth, and a woman was crawling around barking and growling. And in another church a woman at the altar, grunting and groaning, was exorcising a demon. I wouldn't mind casting out some of my demons. But not at the altar. This blessing requires the whole con-gregation to break out with loud laughter every hour or so. No wonder. But the strangest thing is pogoing. I read that a pretty, young woman bounced up and down for more than an hour to band music, proving the power of God. I can see it now on the bumpers, "Pogo if you love Jesus."

No sound of silence or still, small voice will ever be heard in this Tower of Babel where we live.

It will take a worldwide, ear-splitting crack of horrendous thunder to get our attention. And the skies will have to open . . . well, actually, the skies are already open. Maybe somewhere a sun will explode with a blinding light and a more terrifying voice than we can imagine will shout, not "Be still and know that I am God," but "Be still and SHUT UP!"

This morning, before daylight, someone was calling my name. It was not God, but was my husband, Paul, gone from this world twelve years. Once in a while at this time of the day, my mother, my sister Lois, or Paul, all now in that great we-know-not-where, calls to me. I am shocked from dreams and suddenly wide awake, but it is a pleasant thing. Only on these mornings do I ever see the sun rise. I walk around with one of them in the quiet of the morning, waiting for the sun and the coffee.

I am sitting now on the front porch in a heavenly stillness. The only moving thing is the tail of a wren in the sage. The western sky above the hills is pale pink and the white limestone cliffs across Lake Travis are turning to gold. Mysterious purple clouds and mists are hanging low over the water in the bend of the lake, as in a Japanese painting. So I am sitting here in a perfect repose, sorting out my soul, waiting and listening for God. I don't hear him. I hear a little tree frog.

Is that you, God?